I'D LIKE TO PLAY ALONE, PLEASE

I'D LIKE TO PLAY ALONE, PLEASE

 ESSAYS

TOM SEGURA

GRAND CENTRAL
PUBLISHING

NEW YORK   BOSTON

Grand Central Publishing
Hachette Book Group
1290 Avenue of the Americas, New York, NY 10104
grandcentralpublishing.com
twitter.com/grandcentralpub

First edition: June 2022

Grand Central Publishing is a division of Hachette Book Group, Inc. The Grand
Central Publishing name and logo is a trademark of Hachette Book Group, Inc.

The publisher is not responsible for websites (or their content) that are not owned
by the publisher.

The Hachette Speakers Bureau provides a wide range of authors for
speaking events. To find out more, go to www.hachettespeakersbureau.com
or call (866) 376-6591.

Library of Congress Cataloging-in-Publication Data has been applied for.

ISBNs: 9781538704639 (hardcover), 9781538704622 (ebook)

Printed in Canada

MRQ-T

10   9   8   7   6   5   4   3   2   1

For Dad

Contents

A Note from the Author

When Jeffrey Epstein called me in the summer of 2013, I didn't know what to make of it. We had spent time together in Paris the prior spring.

Kidding! Just checking that you're actually reading this.

No, but seriously. This book is intended to reframe the human experience. Where Stephen Hawking's *A Brief History of Time* fell short, this book, quite simply, delivers. You're about to read a remarkable piece of work. Not a single other person on this planet could do this, because I have a unique set of skills. Those skills are, but not limited to, a fair but not superb grasp of the English language. I speak it fluently but am not aware of a single grammatical rule. I graduated high school with a 2.1 GPA. It's the .1 I want you to focus on. It really highlights the fighter in me. I could have sunk, but I knew to come up for air and get that .1 in my pocket. I'm also, depending on who you ask, *very* funny or not funny *at all*. Reading the book will help you decide. I underwent three major operations during the writing of this book, four if you count the vasectomy (major because my balls are).

The important thing to remember is this: This is nonfiction.

I didn't make any of it up. I also didn't change anyone's name to protect them. I did the opposite. If I have a photo of them, it's in here.

One other thing: Are the Taliban really *that* bad? Seems like they're a bunch of knuckleheads, but mostly the kind of guys you want to have a beer with.

My Father, the Savage

"Hello," I answered my phone.

"Heyyyy, buddy!" It's my father's familiar greeting. Since I was a child, I've been "buddy" to him. His pitch goes up, the way your voice does when you greet a little kid. He almost always sounds like he can't believe I answered. "I can't talk right now," he continued.

"You called *me*."

Nothing is as equally frustrating and recognizable as my dad's absolutely insane social skills. The way he navigates phone calls and conversations in general, I have no idea how he operates in the world, never mind how he once held down a high-level corporate job.

Where was he going with this?

"I'll call you back." Silence.

Did that exchange seem odd to you? Well, it seems on par for me. Normal, even, if you know my dad. Ret. Marine Corps Capt. Thomas N. Segura. We have different middle names, so I'm not a junior—something he's pointed out to me, his own son, no less than four thousand times. Almost everyone who has spent any significant time with my father has a similar story about him: "We were in the middle of a conversation and then...he just walked away." Keep in mind that he doesn't excuse himself. There's no "I'll be right back." My dad will just walk away from what you would perceive as a "hang," or he'll hang up the phone during a "conversation" by injecting a simple "Okay, I gotta go." The phone part he usually does once he's done talking and now you are the one sharing something with him, like a thought, a concern, or a story. I wish there were an easy explanation for this, like a developmental or behavioral issue. It isn't either of those things. He knows that we all share virtually the same experience with him.

"I get bored and I don't waste my time once I feel that way." *Oh, so we're boring you? Wonderful.*

One spring break during college, I brought my roommates down to Florida, where my parents live, to stay for a few days. One evening, Casey, my 4.0 GPA, super polite, thoughtful roommate, came over to me wide-eyed.

"Hey, man. I don't know what I did, but I think I offended your dad."

"What'd you say?"

"Well, that's just it. I don't know. I was talking to him...and then he just walked away. He's in another room now." I reassured Casey that what he had experienced was *normal* for my dad. When I went to chastise my father, who was by then watching television, he barely registered it. "Oh, well, I was done talking. Watching this now."

At my cousin's recent wedding, a former neighbor who only knew me as a small child told me that at the reception my father did the same to him, only the neighbor laughed. "He hasn't changed one bit!" After all these years I can say that I *almost* admire the way he disengages once the conversation doesn't serve his interests, but I don't. I still get upset, actually. I sometimes let it slide, but every now and then I feel like I have to call him out. To be clear, it still has absolutely *zero* effect on him when I do. What's even more, he likes to say that he's "gotten much better about that." He hasn't. And it doesn't take much to convince him of that either.

"You really haven't gotten better."

"Really?"

"Yeah, really."

"I'm wondering if I have cancellation insurance on the cruise in October."

"What?"

See? He just doesn't stay in the moment—unless it involves his ass.

When my dad isn't walking away from you because he's bored or hanging up the phone because he's not interested in what you have to say, then he is probably going on about something in his digestive tract. Most, and I do mean *most,* of my dad's phone calls and conversations in person and on the phone are about shitting, farting, wiping, or wishing he was doing one of those things. Countless times I have answered my phone and my father starts describing a bowel moment in complete sincerity and without saying hello.

Me: Hello.

My dad: Ya ever get some shit on your hand and then you have to reach back and wipe with the hand you don't normally wipe with? I had one of those today. I gotta get this call. Talk to you later.

This is not a joke to him. To him, bowel movements are not simply a joy, they are criminally underappreciated by the masses, and he has taken it upon himself to spread the good word. He has named himself the head publicist of this cause, and he wants you to listen. If you're not a believer now, please just spend a few minutes listening to my father's convincing pleas. "It's something we all do, but no one wants to talk about it!" is a favorite expression of his. He is making up for literally everyone who doesn't want to talk about the seven different fart smells he recognizes from himself. Each smell, he says, tells him what will happen next. And it's knowing *that* that gives him comfort and security.

"I can tell if I'm gonna be sick or constipated just by my smell." My father also has nicknames for the different bowel movements he produces. "Sloppy Joes," "Number Sevens," and "Cherry Bombs" all mean very specific things to him, and if you spend enough time with him, you can learn all these cool details too! "Cherry Bombs get splatter on the cheeks, Sloppy Joes just kind of fall out of you." He's proud to have these distinctions and happy to discuss any and all of this in detail with anyone. He's told some of his shitting stories so many times that he'll refer to them by their titles: "Orlando Airport," "The Miami Trip," "Lobster." As his son, I know how to crack each code. He shit his pants at the Orlando airport and had to throw out his underwear in the stall. He took, according to him, the biggest shit in the history of mankind on a family vacation in Miami, one that he swears had an adverse effect on his digestive system. Oh, he also shit his pants in the lobby of a hotel after eating lobster once.

If there was one thing I could count on as a constant throughout my childhood, it was the ritual of my dad watching television in bed, wearing his paper-thin boxers. He'd be lying on his side, and from time to time he'd reach back with one hand, grimace, fart, then bring that hand immediately to his nose. "Why are you smelling that hand you farted in?" I must have asked hundreds of times.

"So I can tell what's going on inside of me."

More fun than pointing out what'd he done was pointing it out to my mother, who no doubt had trained herself to ignore what she found repulsive. It was my self-appointed duty to remind her. I loved upsetting her as a child and continue to want to horrify her to this day. Truly, nothing makes me laugh harder than seeing my mother recoil with utter disgust and bewilderment. "Why does it give you pleasure to be so disgusting?" is her mantra with me.

My honest-to-God, hand-on-the-Bible answer is "I don't know." I really don't know why, but I love to see people, and especially my mother, aghast at what I have said or shown them.

My brain registered early on that my mother and father didn't entirely seem like a match. Not the way other parents seemed to be. First of all, there was definitely a communication issue. My mother married my father when she was thirty-one years old. She had spent her first thirty-one years in her native Peru. Her English-speaking level was, in her words, "shit," or "chet," as she would say it. They're both old-school Catholic and often point to that when all their glaring differences come to light: "But we have God." I mean that's great, but shouldn't you line up on a *couple* other interests?

My dad is a barbarian. He was a three-time state champion Olympic weight lifter. As a lieutenant in the Marine Corps, he led a platoon of men in battle in Vietnam (he retired a captain). He loves street jokes. Bad ones. He's basically a savage: burps, farts, chicks, and guns.

My mother married him as a virgin. I'm sorry I know that. She came from an era and a place where that wasn't unusual. She prays the rosary anytime a car ride lasts longer than ten minutes. She likes petting dogs, playing bridge, and worrying a lot out loud. She has exemplary manners. She's anxious, paranoid, and often hilarious. She's legit funny. Some people are just born with it. She knows how to tell a story; she knows to build tension, exaggerate certain details, add color to characters, and give commentary throughout the story. She honestly does it much better than a lot of comedians I know.

As a kid I put together that my mother would disassociate when my father was being gross. She would either physically leave the room, distract herself, or, my favorite, yell at him. Whenever I was in the same room as the two of them and he was doing something repulsive, I felt the urge to point it out. I *wanted* her to notice. This way I could see the disturbed expression creep onto her face and maybe get one of her hilarious verbal rants going.

"Did you see what Dad just did?"

"Ay!" she would say in her heavily accented English. "Iz so deesgusting! Tom, please! Animals don't do what you are doing."

If you think that unsolicited conversations about farts and shits are the *only* thing my father talks about, you would be gravely mistaken. He's also a big, BIG fan of talking about war. All wars are a thrill to talk about, but the Vietnam war is the one my father participated in, and he will talk about its atrocities without warning, with a straight face, like he's mentioning which barbecue place makes the best coleslaw. Some vets need to feel comfortable with people to be willing to share stories of the most traumatic experience of their lives with them. My dad just needs you to be near him. I've introduced friends to my father, and within moments: "So we're coming over hill sixty-five, and let me tell ya something, the Vietcong were known for mines. We come down the hill and *boom*, guy next to me stepped on a mine. Lost both legs and his torso is blown wide open."

"Uh, Dad. I think the server is waiting for us to order."

As I've gotten older he's shared more and more about the war. I can't imagine what it's like to keep that stuff inside. It's without question one of the worst things a human being can experience, and I'm certain it forever changes who you are. I'm glad he feels comfortable enough to continue telling these stories. His timing, though, is almost always odd. Many car rides with him have bouts of complete silence and then, "A fifty-millimeter gun is really a game changer. We knew the enemy was over this bridge and they thought they were safe. Didn't know we had a fifty on us. With a fifty, you can hit someone in the shoulder—dead. Let's stop for gas soon, buddy."

No person or setting is too sacred for my dad's death stories. We once got together for a rare extended family gathering. Cousins, uncles, and aunts were seated and eating. My father actually waited until people were settled in before he decided to bring up what a "sucking chest wound" is. "Sometimes when a guy is shot in the chest it'll create a hole in his lungs and their lungs can collapse from the added pressure or they'll just take blood in through the wound and drown in their own blood."

Care to pass the mashed potatoes?

War stories are one of the few things my dad actively tries to shield my mom from. I don't know why he thinks she can't handle them but a stranger can. I do my best to get those stories into my mother's head, once again, to upset her. I also love telling her about horrific crimes I hear on the news. The more disturbing, the better. The goal has always been and continues to be to get my mother to react the same way she did when I was a kid and had just pointed out that my dad had smelled his own fart: physical repulsion followed by verbal displeasure. "Ay, Tommy, why? Why does it make you happy to be this way?"

It just does.

I should note that even with all his talk of bowel movements and brutal war stories, the *savage* I call "dad" was as tender and gentle as they come. He always said "I love you" and always hugged and kissed me. He died just weeks after this manuscript was handed in, after a long battle with cancer. I'll never get to hear another story about farts or Nam. No more absurd phone calls that just end without warning. Days before he passed, he asked me if I knew what happens after someone dies.

"What?"

"The world goes on."

Paging Dr. Stupid

I didn't always think I'd be a comedian. There was a time when I was fairly certain I'd be a doctor. Before you say, "Uh, I've been reading this book and I've seen your stand-up, and if there's one thing I'm certain of, it's that you don't come from doctor stock," I'll tell you to stop being so *rude* for a second because, actually, I do.

Both of my great-grandfathers on my father's side were doctors. My great-uncle on the same side was an ophthalmologist. My mother's father was a revered obstetrician; his brother was a surgeon. My dad's brother, Joe, was a world-renowned urologist; his daughter, Leal, is an anesthesiologist. My cousin Suzanna is an infectious disease specialist, and just for good measure, cousin Marisol is a veterinarian. You get the idea. There are a *lot* of smart people in my family on both sides.

I am not one of them.

The evidence was there from an early age. For example, in fifth grade we were given an eight-week-long science project assignment. I went home and told my parents. "I have to do a science project over the next eight weeks. Not sure what to do."

My dad, also not a doctor, jumped right in.

"Why don't you take pictures of the sun at the same time once a week. You'd show how the earth tilts with your pictures. That'd be neat."

"Uh...okay."

We took our first picture that day, the next week another one. Soon, six weeks had gone by and our science teacher started checking in with the class.

"How's everyone's projects coming along? You'll be presenting them in two weeks."

Kids started chiming in about ideas that were, frankly, *wild* to my ears.

"My sea level rise projections are where I'd thought they'd be."

"I'm a little surprised at the concentration of volcanic ash that I'm seeing."

What the fuck?!

Sea levels? Ash? I'm taking pictures *of the sun*! I played it cool because I was too embarrassed to admit I was out of my element, but I was also stunned. How were these *kids* coming up with this stuff? How were they even discussing these things in such scientific detail? Was I really just dumb and not aware of it?

The teacher gave us each a large piece of cardboard with a fold on either side, like a giant pamphlet, to use for our presentation. The pamphlet was displayed upright so everyone could see the details of your project. You basically used the whole canvas to tell the story of your hypothesis, the experiment, and the outcome.

The project was due on the Monday directly following the Super Bowl. Earlier in the week my mother had the photos developed, and I began working on placing them on the cardboard *during* the game. Later, I learned this was a big mistake. The other kids had actually been spending weeks and significant time getting theirs ready. I don't remember exactly what my hypothesis was, but it was probably something like, "All my pictures of the sun will prove that Earth is really spinning," or something worse. I do remember what my big piece of cardboard looked like. Like medical school was not in my future. I have terrible handwriting, and this cardboard was *filled* with it. The photos of the sun? They were taped and glued all over the board with no thought for symmetry or design. My conclusion? *The Earth did indeed move.*

I knew that it looked like shit, but I must have thought that other kids would have shitty presentations too. Sure, they were discussing more advanced theories, but why would they be artistically gifted in how they presented those ideas? Well, they were. Not one looked like mine. Not. One.

The school gym had been converted into a science fair auditorium. Banners hung with depictions of the moon or chemistry elements. It was very clear, today was about science. When I put my poster board on the display table, I looked over at another kid's and immediately folded mine closed. What was happening? They were all written in beautiful fonts. They used multiple colors and typed up their hypotheses. Some even had interactive props. *Props!* The volcano kid? He had a little volcano in the middle of his display that was oozing out fake lava. Another kid had wildlife sounds playing from a speaker as you looked at her project about the Amazon River. It looked like it could be in the Smithsonian.

No one said anything to me about my project, but they didn't need to. It was all in their eyes. The teachers, the other kids, their parents. I saw the way they looked at my project with the type of pitying glance usually reserved for when you see a homeless person sitting outside a Michelin-starred restaurant. My head hung low. I was mortified at how bad my presentation was, but the worst was still to come.

After all the projects were reviewed and everyone was able to take a good, long look at my terrible work, the teachers presented the students with ribbons. The ribbons were gold, red, or blue. Each one had "1st," "2nd," or "3rd" printed on it. It took me a minute to realize they weren't awarding a ribbon to *only* the first-, second-, and third-place projects, but that all the students were getting a ribbon, meaning there were multiple ribbons awarded for each place. I took a deep, relieved breath.

I guess third place isn't so bad.

I walked around the gym taking in all the far better projects. I saw all the proud faces and all the red, blue, and gold ribbons, but when I returned to my poster board I saw something I didn't see anywhere else: a *green* ribbon. Upon closer inspection I could see that this was not first, second, or third place. This one said something else: "Participation Award." And yes, it was the only one given out.

It was absolutely humiliating.

Luckily, I was dumb enough that not even this made me realize how dumb I was. I kept the dream of being a doctor going.

Two years later, I overheard that a heart attack was actually something called coronary thrombosis. This made me *very* excited. I'm good with memorization, and I do especially well with words and phrases that others struggle to say. As a seventh grader, I beamed. *What an excellent term.* I told my teacher I wanted to be a cardiothoracic surgeon. I thought that sounded really smart. I overenunciated it in an extra effort to impress.

"Car-dee-oh-thur-ass-ick" surgeon.

His eyes popped.

"*Oh my.* That's excellent that you know what you want to do. Such an impressive field."

His approval was all I needed. I was ready to announce I'd be a doctor again. When other kids would talk about the jobs they wanted to pursue I'd nod, considering their clearly inferior choices, before I revealed my impressive career plan, saying "cardiothoracic surgeon" with just enough of a hint of arrogance to suggest I might be able to do it. Little did they know I wouldn't even pass basic math classes, but that was yet to come.

During my freshman year of high school I pitched my history teacher on a topic for my term paper: the history of surgery. I'd really wow them there. I'd not only blow people's minds by exploring such a fascinating topic, but I'd also learn so much about my future profession: a win-win.

My idea was to research when the first documented surgeries took place and tell the story of how they evolved, ending with today's modern medical world. My uncle Joe got me the hookup. I'd tail surgeons for an entire day at the Mayo Clinic in Jacksonville to see what the latest procedures were. I couldn't wait to gather all this information so I could present my paper and solidify my pathway, my birthright, to becoming Dr. Thomas Segura, MD.

Surgery starts early. This would be my first red flag for this career. They were performing their first procedure at 7:15 a.m. I feel like sitting up straight at 7:15 a.m. is a challenge. These guys are performing surgery. A resident told me I'd be shadowing thirteen different procedures that day. The surgeon pulled me and my father aside before the first one. My dad had accompanied me, as he was curious about all of this too. We were about to enter the operating room.

"The lady in there is awake, just so you know. She's numb below her waist, but she's not asleep, so just don't say anything about, you know..."

My father, who at the time was in corporate finance, said without hesitation:

"Her pussy."

JEEZUS, dude! I looked at him in disbelief.

Did my dad really just say that?

But much to my surprise, the surgeon nodded.

"Exactly. It's not going to...look good."

He was not lying.

The poor lady was eighty-four, and her legs were wide open. My father and I, who she must have assumed were medical staff since we wore scrubs, masks, and even gloves, hovered over the surgeon's shoulder. He sat, well, as close to her vagina as you'd need to to do what he was about to do. It should be noted that this was the first vagina I ever saw in person, and it made me think, *Maybe these aren't for me.*

The doctor used a device to pry her vaginal walls open, he got a bunch of lube on his hands, and then he went in, with his whole hand. My dad and I looked at each other. This was awfully awkward father–son bonding. He stared at me for a bit, and I knew what he was thinking. He wanted to say something awful about her pussy. My look communicated something back to him: "I know what you want to say, Dad. Don't."

The doctor used the device to spread her even further open, and then his hand pulled something toward her opening. It was a softball-size cyst that was still attached to her.

"Grab the camera. This is incredible."

One of his staff took off and returned quickly with a large

Canon camera. He was thrilled. "This has to be a record-size vaginal cyst."

They snapped pictures and then they ruptured the cyst. An endless flow of pus streamed out of it. The medical staff let her know what they were doing and how remarkable it was.

"This won't be bothering you anymore, ma'am."

Let me remind you that I'm witnessing all of this as a fourteen-year-old kid. It was pretty advanced stuff. As we left the operating room, I took a deep breath and turned to my dad.

"We have twelve more of these today." My dad nodded and then leaned in to my ear.

"Can you imagine what it smells like between her legs?"

Very cool comment, Dad!

We spent the next nine hours in and out of every possible procedure on gallbladders, urethras, testicles, kidneys, and at least one more older vagina. I wasn't yet totally aware that I didn't have the brain to do what these people were doing, but I did leave there with certainty that I didn't want to do this for a living. This would be the day that I told myself and my father.

"I don't want to be a doctor."

"That's okay, buddy." His support meant a lot. I know that part of me wanted to do it to make him proud.

"It's important to try things, and you'll figure out what you want to do over time."

But a new path was already clear to me. I wanted to play football in the NFL.

Bruce Bruce

Delta 1701, LAX to ATL, 9:06 a.m.

When I spotted XXXL comedian Bruce Bruce at the gate in Los Angeles, I did what I almost always do when I see a celebrity. I think, *Oh, there's that person I recognize. I'm not going to do anything about it.* I really hate bothering people, and unless I see an opening that will aggravate minimally, I don't say shit to anyone. I should mention that my wife and I were both on this flight, but only I was upgraded to first class. I could have done a few things here: tell the airline I don't want my upgrade as I'd rather sit in coach next to my wife (nope!) *or* give my upgrade to my wife. What I did do was offer the upgrade to her, but she insisted that I enjoy it (later, she would give me shit about not coming back enough to check on her, but that's another story!).

When I got to my seat and noticed Bruce Bruce was seated directly across the aisle from me, I took it as a sign that I should say something. Bruce Bruce is a killer. In the world of stand-up comedy, that's a good thing. You want people to refer to you as one, and I was certain I was sitting next to one. I'd been familiar with him for years from his time on BET and numerous other TV appearances. He was a staple at all the big-time comedy clubs, always selling out shows and getting rave reviews. You can look him up online or, better yet, go to a show. The guy *murders*. I introduced myself and told him that I was also a comic. As terrible as some comics are when it comes to personality and character, 99 percent have an opening in their hearts, however brief, for kindness, decency, perhaps just a moment of graciousness when someone else mentions that they too are a comic. It's a fraternity. No matter what you're doing, if a stranger approaches and says, "I'm a comic," you stop, say hello, and perhaps buy them a drink or more. When I said I was a comic to Bruce Bruce, I saw the switch flip. He lit up. Immediately we started sharing stories of shows, our favorite cities, comics, and places to eat. It was everything I could have wanted in that moment.

"We are going to be delayed while mechanics address a light displayed during routine preflight checks. You can get off the plane if you'd like; just bring your boarding pass with you," the flight attendant announced on a five-times-louder-than-necessary PA system. Normally, that's the worst thing you can hear, but I was lost in conversation with the great Bruce Times Two. I suppose I could have used this time to tell Bruce I needed to go back and check on my wife and see if she wanted to get off the plane, but this was way more fun than doing that.

As our chat continued, people began taking the flight attendant's offer and leaving the plane. One passenger who was making her way up the aisle to deboard stopped right in between Bruce and me and asked with what appeared to be a familiar tone, "Is there anything you want or need?"

Bruce thought for a beat. "Candy."

"Candy?" She seemed to be looking for some direction.

"Twix, Skittles, shit like that."

She nodded and walked off. "Who is that?" I assumed it was his assistant, but he shook his head. "I don't know." This was a level of fame I was yet unfamiliar with. "Are *strangers* buying you candy?" My voice raised higher than normal because I was genuinely impressed. He smiled and nodded proudly. Unreal.

Bruce next talked about a comic who he felt disrespected him on a show. It was something every comedian is familiar with: a guy ignoring the light and just staying up there as long as he pleased. It's a major faux pas in stand-up. It's selfish. Like ordering a sharing plate at a restaurant and eating everything on it while your friends stare. Yes, I've done that before.

Bruce and I were talking shop and I *loved* it. We started listing our favorite comics ever, and it was like a history class. Lenny Bruce, Dick Gregory, Carlin, Pryor, and so on. When the list rounded up, Bruce Bruce threw this at me: "Do you know who the funniest cat of all time is?" It's the type of question that gives you pause. *Did we skip someone?* was my first thought. Then it hit me. It was a setup. He was asking so I'd say, "Who?" and then he could say that *he* was the funniest cat of all time. I have to admit—I loved it. Loved that he was going to boast and I was going to eat it up. So I smiled and said, "Who?"

"Andy Griffith," Bruce said with a dead-ass serious look on his face.

"Huh?"

Bruce nodded this time as if to affirm what he already knew to be true. "Andy. Griffith." I was so confused, I couldn't tell if this was a bit, so I started to whistle in an attempt to clarify, at least to me, that we were talking about the same guy. Bruce, once again, nodded.

"You ever been to the Andy Griffith museum before?" he asked as if that wasn't the single craziest question I'd ever heard.

"No. Is that real?"

"Real?! You can sit in the car he used to sit in and you can touch shit that he used to touch." There it was. You make assumptions about people all the time, only to be surprised by who they are. Clearly, Bruce Bruce, the notable, accomplished, three-hundred-plus-pound Black comedian, is a die-hard Andy Griffith fan.

"You ever see episode two fifteen of the *Andy Griffith Show*?" I swear to you I looked around the cabin hoping another passenger was hearing this absurd question. He asked as if I not only was familiar with the show, but would be able to recall episodes by their air date codes *from memory*. "No, I think I missed that one." He barreled forward. "That's my favorite episode. It originally aired March 13, 1967." How could this be real? It was.

"'Opie's Piano Lesson.'" He knew the name of the episode. *Bananas.*

The woman who had spoken to him earlier returned with both Twix *and* Skittles, and Bruce offered her a "Thank you, darling." He turned to me again and smiled as he raised his sugar treats as if to toast, "All right, man," and he got to snacking. That was it. Conversation over. We had four hours of flying time for me to contemplate the comedic mastery of Andy Griffith.

Twix. Skittles. Shit like that.

I Had a Dream

August 17, 2014, should have been an ordinary day for me. I'd slept in a little, drank some coffee, and, to my surprise, found a voice mail waiting for me. I know getting a voice mail shouldn't be a surprise, but I had AT&T back then. Almost everywhere I went in Los Angeles, my service was complete dog shit. I hope John Stankey, the CEO of AT&T (as of this writing), is reading this. Your cell service sucks a dead dog's dick on a dusty driveway. I have dreams of murdering my phone almost daily. Back in 2014, most people who came over to my place would get surprise voice mails popping up on *their* phones because most people who came over had either Sprint or Verizon Wireless. I had a few poor friends who had T-Mobile, and their phones would just automatically shut off. We're no longer friends (they were *really* poor!). For a short while, when I lived in a guest house in Redondo Beach, having AT&T was like having a satellite phone at the White House. No dropped calls. So why didn't my phone ring on this morning? To this day there's no good explanation. It was just meant to be. At the time I didn't realize it, but getting the voice mail was better than getting the phone call. The voice mail was *proof.* It was the culmination of my life's work. All my childhood fantasies (okay, not *all*, but a lot) came true that day.

I pressed play. " 'Sup, Tom! This is Big Daddy Kane…"

For a lot of us who grew up in suburban America in the 1980s and '90s, hip-hop was an obsession. It exploded rapidly in popularity, and with good reason. It was cool, and we weren't. When you're a young man, you take your cues from the men around you. They help shape who you become, but have you been to the suburbs? Bland. That's basically the definition of the 'burbs. It's slower and safer and there's not a lot of *flavor*. You learn how to act, dress, and talk from the guys that surround you. The guys that surrounded me taught me I'm supposed to part my hair with a comb, wear khakis, and always reply with "I am *well*," when someone asks me how I'm doing. So, when I heard hip-hop for the first time, I thought, *This is the SHIT!* It was like a portal into a world my friends and I didn't know existed. It was exciting and flashy and dangerous and really just cool as *fuck*! These are the guys you wanted to be like, dress like, talk like.

This is around the time when I started playing sports as a kid. Football and basketball were my two favorites. Now that I had acquired these passions, I felt like I was set. I imagined I was *so* unique. And, of course, I was. A young white kid who listens to hip-hop all day and then gets really into pro football and basketball. Have you ever heard of such a thing?

It's no secret that if you're *really* into those particular sports and that music, you are being heavily influenced by Black guys. I thought it was great. Hell, I wanted to *be* Black. If you're thinking, *Oh, really? You want to be racially profiled and discriminated against and have to work twice as hard for half the recognition, or you just want the good stuff that you see glamorized on television?*

No, of course I don't want the terrible parts. I just want the cool, glamorized stuff. I want the cool haircuts like high-top fades and dreads. I want the gold chains and the forty-four-inch vertical and the dance moves. How many cool AF dance moves can this group of people come up with? That's the stuff I want. I know how that sounds, but it's the truth.

Today's socially aware, hyperwoke crowd surely wants to lecture me and maybe you about it. "You're appropriating Black culture," read one tweet to Kim Kardashian. Uh, that's *one* way of putting it! Am I right? Anyone? Kim has a big ass and fucks Black dudes. I don't know that it's fair to say that she's appropriating Black culture. Maybe you can say she fetishizes it? Look, she definitely likes Black guys, and they seem to really like her too. It's almost too perfect how they found each other. It seems like her ass has a lot to do with it, but that invites another stereotype: Black guys love big asses. Am I saying that Black dudes love big asses and Kim *grew* one in the hope of luring them into her large, Armenian turd churner? Maybe? By the way, I also *love* big asses. Does that make me *not white*?

But *America* as a whole, particularly White America, we are *guilty* of said charge. We take and take and exploit and profit from the works of others. It's nothing new. We "found" this land that other people lived on and took that shit too.

White people—we're just a good time!

It's hard to argue that there's "appreciation" and then there's taking what isn't yours without so much as a "please" or "thank you." Q-Tip of the mighty Tribe Called Quest lectured Iggy

Azalea about it. Jesse Williams at the BET awards said we "gen-trify" Black genius. That's so on point it should be on a monu-ment. And nothing about it is recent. White people stole the blues, rock 'n' roll, and tried our best to take hip-hop. It sounds like a hack premise to a joke you've already heard, but does that make it any less true? Some people are tired of it and don't want to hear it, but that's just more reason to get into it. Let's just be real here: Black people and Black culture are dope. Call it what you want, I think Diddy calls it Black *excellence*. Sounds right to me.

I began my own love affair with Black American culture when I was really young. At eight years old I was hanging out with my next-door neighbor, Dan Cote. Dan had exceptional musical taste even as a child (he would later go on to work in a record store and even manage musicians). He made me watch *The Breakfast Club* (the movie) and told me to pay attention to Judd Nelson's "per-formance." What nine-year-old talks like that? We also used to watch the Spice channel, waiting for those few happy moments it wasn't scrambled and we'd masturbate next to each other in sleep-ing bags thinking the other didn't know what was going on. But back to his taste.

Dan was a year older than me. Here's a nine-year-old that would play the Smiths, Pink Floyd, the Beatles, and at the time a good bit of hair metal too. Mötley Crüe, Def Leppard, all the big rock bands of the eighties. It was fine, but it didn't *move* me. There's music you don't mind hearing and then there's music that grabs you by your balls or your heart or both! Don't get me wrong, I liked *some* of the popular rock stuff. You could *pour some sugar on me* and *welcome me to your jungle* and I'd hap-pily *enter, sandman* with you. Some of it was cool and I dug those tracks.

But when I heard the Fat Boys, it was *over.* Just to be clear, this is way before I was fat. I saw those dudes and I *wished* I were fat. Black, of course. But these dudes even made being *fat* seem cool. The white rockers I didn't really *get.* I didn't get big hair, sleeveless leather vests with hoop earrings, and shouting that sounded like screeching. But funky bass lines with Kangols, talking shit, and eating food? That seemed right where I wanted to be. The Fat Boys were three young Black dudes from Brooklyn who entertained the hell out of my young, impressionable mind. They could beatbox, which might as well be magic, especially to a kid, *any* kid. It doesn't seem like the sounds they're generating are possible. You're hearing drums, record scratches, and electronic distortion, and it's just this dude doing it with *his mouth*!

I'd eventually get into Doug E. Fresh, Biz Markie, and Rahzel as well, but the Fat Boys were my first loves. On top of being super talented, the Fat Boys were also funny. They even did a goofy, screwball comedy called *Disorderlies* that when I was a kid I thought was *Citizen Kane.* I thought every kid must have loved these dudes. I wanted to hang out with them and be one of them.

I was completely in love with hip-hop, but I have to admit that I didn't grasp all the slang. So what did I do? Well, I went to the library, of course. I mean, if you were curious about a subject or topic that you didn't fully comprehend, wouldn't you go to the library too? Luckily for me, the library had a book about hip-hop that, in retrospect, appeared to be written by and for a profoundly stupid person or maybe just a child. What I remember is that it seemed like it was written by someone not at all steeped in real hip-hop culture. Looking back, it *must* have been written by a white person. But I didn't know any better: All I saw was that Run-DMC was on the cover and the book had a large glossary of slang words and their definitions—exactly what I needed. With my new hip-hop guide I would be fully informed and know exactly how to *kick it with the fellas* on the corner. And by *fellas* I mean other students going to Sacred Heart Elementary, and by the *corner* I mean waiting for the school bus.

The passive knowledge I got from reading this book sent me on my way to being an expert, but it wasn't enough. I mean, I did learn to greet people by saying "Yo" and depart by saying "Peace," but I wanted more. I needed to *show* people, especially my family, that hip-hop and I were *one*. Fortunately for me, evidence of what I'm about to tell you no longer exists, but if I were on the witness stand in a court of law I would swear that this is the truth. I used the slang that I learned in the book to write my own rhymes. I'm cringing so hard as I type this that I think I might pass out. It's completely embarrassing, and yet I have to confess it. I not only wrote rhymes in a journal, I performed them for anyone who would listen. I was looking to teach those who hadn't heard yet that this rap thing was pretty neato! I hadn't learned to memorize my rhymes, so like a real savant I'd ask the person, "Would you like to hear some rap?" And then they would probably go, "Uh, okay."

Great.

Let me just get my journal out and spit some bars for you.

> *My name is Tom and I'm so def*
> *When I write rhymes I use my left*
> *I'm not trippin' cause I'm fresh*
> *All you bustas gonna see what's next.*

So you can see I was a natural MC. I basically tried to shoehorn all the slang I read in the book into every line, and then I would not know how to use some of it, so I would just drop it in *wherever* in the hope that using *so many* slang terms would mask that I didn't really know what I was saying, and people would think, *Wow, this kid really knows how to rap!* For the better part of a year I subjected people to my sick rhymes. I thought I was pretty clever and talented at it, so I was sure they did too.

But nobody ever said that to me. My dad would stare, stone-faced, waiting for it to make sense to him—kind of like one of those paintings at the mall where you zone out looking at one image and then another image pops out at you. My mother's English wasn't the best to begin with, and here I was saying "word" but not using its common definition. Instead, I was saying "word" the way my favorite rappers were using it, as a term of acknowledgment or con-firmation. So when my mom would say, "Tommy, dinner is ready." I would reply, "Word."

To a foreigner who is trying to master our language, this defies logic, and I found myself repeatedly making my mother's head explode with confusion.

"What *word*?"

"What?"

"Did I use the wrong word?"

"No...just. I was saying 'word,' you know, 'cause that's what some people...in the hood."

"Are you on drugs?!"

I truly didn't understand anyone, especially a white person, who didn't love Black entertainment as much as I did. *Why didn't my father click with N.W.A or EPMD?* He was a finance guy. Was *Strictly Business* over his head? Didn't he also hate when he said to *"suck the mutha fucka and she bitin' it"*? (RIP, Eazy-E.)

My favorite white guy who surely didn't get it was my

fifth-grade math teacher, Mr. Knurr. He was bald but still rocked the horseshoe and of course, as a math guy, what hair he had was long. His breath was so pungent I can still smell it today. He was a white, white guy. Super white. So it must have come as some surprise the year I wore my *Public Enemy: Fear of a Black Planet* t-shirt to school. I wore the shirt every week. I still have it. I can still see Mr. Knurr's confused face, slowly mouthing the words "Fear...of...a...Black...Planet," then asking me what it meant.

"Public Enemy" was my response. He'd act like that was sufficient, even though I clearly didn't understand what the shirt meant. I just knew that I listened to Public Enemy without fully grasping their message—and I loved it. It must have seemed to him that I was surrendering to Chuck D's message, that I was embracing an undeniable truth: Black people would soon take over and white people were living in fear of it, but I don't think he thought that deeply. You know, *math guy.*

My love of hip-hop and sports took over my perception of everything in the nineties. I thought Georgetown was an all-Black university. If you're nodding at that, I salute you. Back then the Hoyas were a staple on TV because of their basketball team. I was only aware of John Thompson, Mourning, AI, and so on. I never knew it was a predominantly white, well-to-do university in the *very white* Georgetown neighborhood only a few minutes' drive from some of the poorest Black neighborhoods in America.

I can't talk about this topic without mentioning my biggest influence, the mayor of Black entertainment, Deion Sanders. I'm a die-hard FSU football fan. I have trouble remembering the exact moment it happened, but I recall being mesmerized by Sanders— watching in awe as he *flew* by the opposing team, high-stepping and then dancing after scoring. And then after the game he's wearing forty gold chains and driving off in a convertible. Let me remind you that he was in *college* at the time! How could a young man *not* want to *be* that? As far as I was concerned, when I was nine years old, I felt like white dudes were really dropping the ball on showing their youth how to have fun. These Black guys all looked like they were having *fun*. BYU football didn't look fun. FSU, *that* looked fun.

Comedy was the same. Black comedy was sort of exotic in my childhood. It was exciting to drop in on something that wasn't made for me but affected me in such a way that I felt incredibly connected to the performers and the audiences. The topics, the comics, and the audiences almost never had a white person in them, but I wanted to be there. I was laughing so goddamn hard when I watched these shows on TV, I felt like they were calling me. My early influences in comedy are exclusively Black. Bill Cosby (his comedy), Eddie Murphy, Robin Harris, and Martin Lawrence. Thanks to Russell Simmons and HBO I got to sneak into the basement on Saturdays and watch Def Jam, which would expose me to some of the greatest and worst acts ever. I never knew a stool could be used that way!

But the guy who really made me fall in love with comedy was Chris Rock. Every comic has had their moments when they felt like they were funnier than those around them. They usually first happen in school or when hanging out with friends. You think, *I'm different. I have this ability that's tweaked more than everyone else.* For me, I realized I was funny by middle school. I had gone to so many schools because we were always moving, and all these different kids thought I was really funny, so I knew I *must* be. Seeing Chris Rock make people laugh for a living, the way he captivated an audience, made me realize comedy was a viable career option. *That* became my dream.

I held on to that dream throughout school, and soon after graduating college, I found myself in Los Angeles taking improv classes at the Groundlings. Two of my fellow classmates, Sam Tripoli and Nic Wegener—both extremely funny guys who were both stand-ups—pulled me aside and told me I had to try stand-up. Though I hadn't planned on doing it, something in me loved that it was suggested. It was a way to perform without getting the permission you needed, like with acting. I followed those two around for weeks like a lost dog before finally getting the balls to do it. That first time was all I needed. I was hooked. Most comics who stick to doing it have a similar experience. You're either addicted for life or it isn't for you. My first two years, my act was essentially a bad Chris Rock impression. It was so bad. I would pace, crouch, and even gesture with my free hand exactly the way he did. I didn't even realize I was doing it until a couple told me I was "oddly urban" onstage. It was their not-so-coded way of saying, "You sound like you're trying to be Black."

But even though Black comedians influenced my career path, throughout it all, my greatest passion remains the music. The music has and will forever be my lifeline. From Diana Ross and the Supremes to the Juice Crew, SWV to Beyoncé, Bill Withers to Gang Starr, I am and forever will be a someone whose heartbeat is the great music of Black America. It's what I drive to, dance to, chill to, and bang to (not my wife; she prefers French Cafe radio for intimate times, but back in the day I'd drop some D in you to Brian McKnight, En Vogue, you name it).

I believe we all control our own destiny, and if you put

something out in the universe with love and good intentions, some version of what you're looking for will come to you. And for me it kinda did. Eight years after I started doing stand-up I saw Big Daddy Kane getting out of a limousine on Sunset Boulevard and I didn't know what to do with myself. I couldn't wrap my head around what my eyes were seeing.

Big Fuckin' Daddy Kane is...here?!

I was so goddamn excited that I yelled, " 'Sup, Kane!" to get his attention. I should be clear that I did it impulsively and in my best "Black voice." That is to say, the way I've heard countless Black football players yell in my years around the sport. I should also point out—I do that voice *very* well. Kane snapped his head around, looking for who had called out to him, and so naturally I hid behind a wall. I felt extremely stupid for having done it in real life. Moments later, I looked around and he was gone. Years after that I began telling that story onstage, and eventually I did it in my first one-hour special, *Completely Normal.*

Which leads me back to that surprise voice mail I got from Big Daddy Kane. Did you think I was going to leave you hanging about that? The fact that BDK saw my special where I talked about him and ended up calling me made me feel like I had won an award or championship. Not like an award at school. I mean like an Oscar or a Super Bowl. I felt like a goddamn winner, like I had *arrived.* It was as if he was saying to me, "I see you. We all see you." I not only got a message from Kane telling me he saw my bit talking about him and that it made him laugh, but to keep going and push further. It was the kind of encouragement you want to hear from someone you look up to. Later that day I met him at my friend Russell Peters's house. We even came up with a shirt with both of our images on it and marketed it together. It was a dream come true. But what I really took from the whole encounter was *put yourself out there*. If you love barbecue, tell the world. If you love tennis, tell the world. If you love dressing up like a dog and having a dildo that's made to look like a tail inserted into you rectally, tell the world. The world hears you. You'll see.

Overjoyed to meet Big Daddy Kane.

Que Viva El Perú, Carajo!

I speak Spanish. Not like you, you fucking gringo. I grew up speaking Spanish. And I deserve absolutely no credit whatsoever. My mother immigrated to this country after marrying my father. She was thirty-one and spoke about twenty words in English. I speak Spanish because my mom spoke to us in Spanish, and she did so because twenty words of English can only take you so far.

She didn't always know the word for a lot of things. She called the ceiling fan a "monster" because it made noise and that's the only word she knew for a noise-maker. My mother is not of diminished capacities, but after reading that last sentence I'd have second guesses too. Today she speaks fluent English, albeit with a heavy accent. I'd like to take a moment to tell you that my mother uses the word "retarded" *a lot*. Quite a bit, and so do a lot of native Spanish speakers. They haven't received the North American memo that certain terms are offensive to some, and I really love that about them.

My South American cousins often greet me with a "Hello, *faggot*," which, to be clear, I keep telling them is *not okay*. The reason they don't understand is because the Spanish equivalent, "maricon," is still widely used in *their* social circles. They just don't seem to grasp why my eyes bug out of my head since, you know, we're in public. I think it's important to note that none of these people are bigots. They're kind, loving, thoughtful people who have just never subscribed to the notion that "you can't say that." I wish I were as hardcore as they are, but I'm too immersed in American culture to go as far as they do. If you have a foreign parent or relative you're probably nodding right now. You know how hard people outside of America flex their "I really don't give a fuck" mentality. These days it's especially refreshing and so goddamn funny.

From the time I was nine, I would spend my summers in Peru. Not simply vacationing, I would live with family and often go to school there. Our summers are their winters, so when you go down in June, you're not on vacation at all. They're in the middle of their school year. School was an all-boys Catholic school in Lima, Peru. If you don't know what I look like, well, I don't look like I belong. I have very fair skin and blue eyes. It sort of screams gringo, and the kids knew right away that a mark was on campus. It took some balls to go to Peru as an adolescent and look these kids in the eye in order to earn their respect. They all assumed that I was an uppity Yankee they could intimidate. In all my years of going to different schools in different cities, I always stood up to bullies. Not always on day one, but eventually I was going to get their respect.

In a city like Lima and a country like Peru, it's quite the experience to look and feel like an outsider everywhere. Normally you might feel like an outsider when traveling, but you're usually only in one place for a short period of time. If you're a white American in Tokyo, chances are you're only there for a week or two. (Of course, we all understand that some people are there for much longer, like the rest of their lives. That's not who I'm talking about here.) Most of us experience that feeling of being "other" for a fleeting moment. This was not the case for me in Peru. I was there for months at a time.

I had somebody yell in my face "Go home, Yankee!" I had a gun pointed at me. That one was kind of my fault. It wasn't a robbery. It was an armed bodyguard and I knew him. I knew where he was posted. My uncle was highly prominent and had massive political influence at the time. It was not unusual for people in his position to have round-the-clock security. I had gone on a walk after school with my cousin, whose father was the one protected by this guard. We went down to a corner convenience store, like a bodega, and bought ourselves ice cream treats. On our walk back I noted to myself that the armed bodyguard I regularly spoke with was posted up behind a partition that blocked our view of him and his of us. Without telling my cousin, I came up with a plan in my mind that I was sure was going to result in hilarity. I would approach the partition and then jump suddenly to the other side where the bodyguard was, and he would scream, and then we would all laugh at how frightened he was. Sounds funny, right?

Here's how it actually went down. I walked up to the partition, and without telling my cousin I suddenly jumped to the other side where the bodyguard was seated. As I jumped I also let out a scream—the kind of yelling you do on Halloween, you know, monster sounds, like a ceiling fan.

"Rarrrrrrrr!"

I landed from the jump with my arms up in the air and a crazy look on my face. Ice cream was dripping down one hand and of course my screaming continued. Without any hesitation the bodyguard pointed a shotgun at my chest from less than five feet away. Now my monster sounds changed in pitch. They became more of a falsetto screech. I ran!

After I regained my ability to speak, he and my cousin both let me know in no uncertain terms that it was a miracle that I wasn't dead. It's true. They were right. And let that be a lesson to all of you: Don't try to prank armed bodyguards.

I experienced a lot in my time going to Peru. You're forced to grow up fast in an underdeveloped country. They don't have the same resources, luxuries, or laws that we have here in the United States. There are times when that can be frightening, but as a young teen it can also be quite exciting. You don't think you're going to spend a lot of time in a strip club when you're fourteen, but when you're in Lima, Peru, no one asks for your ID. Driving drunk, throwing eggs at innocent bystanders, terrorism—I experienced all of it before my sophomore year in high school. And no, I'm not joking about terrorism. I spent the entire summer of 1993 in Peru. That also happened to be the most active stretch for the infamous Marxist terrorist group the Shining Path. They spent that summer wreaking havoc and setting off bombs. I am talking *real* bombs here. One night it was 2,000 pounds of dynamite packed into the trunk of a taxi and driven into a building. That was their signature attack during that time, and I was there for it. The force of that particular explosion was so profound that it blasted out a window in the home we were staying in more than two miles from the epicenter. After an episode like that, I thought my parents would want their young, teenage son to come home and be out of harm's way. *Nope*. They weren't even a little bit worried. The morning after that bomb went off I called them, terrified, certain the call would lead to heightened emotions, and a plan would come together to extract me back to the United States. I had just experienced a *terrorist attack* and I was still very much a kid. This stood out as a stark reminder that other parts of the world were dangerous in a way that seemed implausible at the time in the United States. I imagined my parents would become characters from *Mission: Impossible* or the Jason Bourne series, stopping at nothing to retrieve their asset. That is not what happened.

My dad reacted as if I had told him there was a *storm* the night before.

"Oh. How far away? Two miles. Wow. What else is going on?"

Oh, not much. Just the terrorist attack I just finished telling you about. They didn't even consider the idea that I should go back to safety. As much as I like giving them shit about it, I'm actually glad I didn't. Because I fucking love Peru. On top of the culture, family, and love, there's also the food.

A lot of people don't know it, but Peru has long been one of the top gastronomical destinations of the world. People travel there *just* to eat. Many go as far as to say that it is the best culinary destination in the world. I am heavily biased, but I completely agree, since it's the food I've been eating my entire life. It's the home of ceviche, a dish that has been modified and altered in countless delicious ways. But if you want the *real thing* you have to go to Peru. *Lomo saltado, aji de gallina, picarones*—the list goes on and on. Every bite a more sensual experience than the last. It's like the food is dancing in your mouth, and not wedding reception dancing. That's sloppy and gross. I mean professional dancing. Like flamenco dancers at the top of their game. It's beautiful, inspiring; your eyes close and you can feel it. *You're alive.*

Many people are surprised to learn that Peru isn't a homogeneous culture. Huge immigrant populations from China, Japan,

Spain, and more fill the country and give the food its unique style and flavor.

Nobu Matsuhisa, the famed chef and restaurateur who owns and operates countless restaurants branded with his name, made Peru his home for a while. Nobu is widely credited with pioneering Asian–Latin fusion after he left Japan at twenty-four and opened a restaurant in Lima, Peru, combining the foods of both cultures. The result is what I would describe as "Proof of God's existence." It's amazing. Don't believe me? Try it for yourself, and if you don't enjoy it, just know that you are wrong and dumb and people don't like you.

As a kid I couldn't just indulge in their delicious cuisine; I had to learn how to live there. I wasn't just passing through; I was trying to be accepted. I saw it as my birthright to call myself Peruvian. I just needed the people there to feel the same way. The kids at school didn't look at me like I was welcomed, but that was nothing new for me. I'd been a "new kid" at a dozen schools.

In Peru the stakes were much higher than any time I had gone to a new school in the US. One of my first days in class at La Immaculada a teacher noticed as he taught class that I had no paper, no pen, no books in front of me. It's true that you should probably have those things with you when you're in school, but I had just arrived and no one had given me any of these things. I was twelve. What am I supposed to do, head out to Rite Aid in Lima and stock up on supplies?

When the teacher spotted me, he stopped his class and yelled quite loudly, "Alumno! Párate!" which translates to "Student! Stand up!" The direct, abrupt, fierce way in which he yelled this absolutely scared the shit out of me. I felt like I was being tried for crimes against the state. He asked me my name, and I replied in

Spanish. Then he asked why I had no supplies. As I hesitated to explain, the other students chimed in, "Porque es gringo!"

His intensity dropped a notch, but the students began to call out that they had questions for me, and much to my surprise he asked me to stand in the front of the class, facing all the students. I obliged and once again felt like I was on trial, fighting for my life. The kids just barked out questions, and the fun, it seemed, would be in tricking me. They assumed I spoke very little or at least insufficient Spanish. One student asked if I brought my dolls to play with, and I answered back that I didn't, but I'd be happy to play with him if he wore a skirt the next day.

The room *erupted*. This was a game. It was a game of language and wits, and it was going to either earn me respect or bury me. And the distinguished, stern teacher was all about it.

The students kept yelling out questions, and I kept firing back. Finally, a student called out that he had a question, and the teacher told him to ask. The kid yelled out, "How many times a day do you masturbate?" I was certain that the teacher was going to annihilate this kid. Instead he looked at me and lifted his head as if to say, "What's your answer?"

"*Si pienso en tu madre, llego hasta siete. A mí me dicen 'mano muerto.'*" I spat it out so fast it was like the universe answered for me. It wasn't even me.

"If I think about your mother, I can do it seven times. They call me *dead hand*."

That is a Hall of Fame level answer for a twelve-year-old speaking his second language. Seriously. I crushed that room so hard that the teacher came over and hugged me. I had won over the kids in the class. It was like a movie. You know those movies where there's some weird kid and people are mocking him, but he joins the soccer team and scores eleven goals in a game and then people are like, "Wow, he's really good. We should stop being such a dick to him." It was like that, but instead of soccer I had words. That isn't to say that everyone was now a big fan of mine. There were still plenty of kids there who wanted to kick the shit out of me, and a couple even tried. But I had friends now, and that meant if you wanted to kick my ass, you were going to have to kick their asses too.

Use what you have. That's the real lesson. If you have looks, exploit those to your advantage. If you're big and strong, intimidate people and maybe physically assault them if you need to. Me? I'm going to talk shit if you press me. Sometimes I'll come up short, sometimes I'll go too far. But sometimes, like in the classroom that day, I'll fuckin' nail it.

Me, my cousin Rodrigo, and my friend Casey fully committing to supporting Peru's national soccer team.

Chris Tucker

Delta 1022, SFO to LAX, 9:03 a.m.

The night before this flight, I was performing for 20,000 people at the Shoreline Amphitheatre just outside San Francisco. I don't think that's a great size for stand-up. Stand-up is an intimate art form. Two hundred seats is really the best if you want to experience stand-up in its purest form. In a small room you can connect with everyone there. The audience picks up on every nuance of your performance. It's almost like you're at a dinner party. In an amphitheater you're "pressing play" on your act. The space is so massive that the audience watches you on a jumbotron, the same screen they'd watch a football game on in a stadium. It takes some getting used to. This was one of the first times I'd done a show of this size.

Dave Chappelle was the main attraction at the Shoreline, but there were a bunch of comics on before him. The show was so big and long that they split it into two acts with an intermission. Chris Tucker closed out the first half. He crushed. I had the fun of going on *right* before Dave. You know, the last guy of the guys they don't want to see before the guy they really want to see. It kind of, well, wasn't that fun, but we can get into that later.

The next morning, I was at the San Francisco airport, which I have come to despise. You will not arrive or leave on time about 100 percent of the time you fly in to or out of there. It's taken me years to figure out that you must use Oakland's airport when you're visiting SF. Trust your boy, that's a pro tip.

At the gate in San Francisco awaiting my flight to Los Angeles I see that Chris Tucker is seated with headphones on, the universal sign for "don't fucking talk to me." I have immense respect for that, just to be clear. (Pro tip: Wear headphones at the airport and on all flights and just ignore everyone who speaks to you.) I did want to talk to him. I had been a big fan for years and now I had done a show with him, but I wasn't going to break the headphones rule and start a conversation at that moment. That would have gone against everything I believe in.

I boarded first and sat in my seat, 3B, an aisle seat in first class. Who sits directly next to me? Chris Tucker. Even then I didn't feel the opening to engage him, so I didn't. I read a car magazine and thought maybe we'd talk later if there was an appropriate moment. As we took off I was lost in the article I was reading, and then I heard a very distinct voice, *his* voice: "Should I do another *Rush Hour?*"

Go back and read that again if you need to. My first thought was that Chris Tucker was talking on the phone to his agent as our plane was departing SFO and he wanted the man's opinion on whether or not he should do this. Another moment passed, and I thought maybe he was talking to the guy behind me. I had seen him at the gate with another guy, so it'd make sense if they were talking as we flew. Just to confirm what was actually happening,

I looked up, and Chris Tucker was looking directly at me. Keep in mind I was a stranger to him at this point. Chris had left during intermission, so he never saw me. He had no idea we had done a show together the night before, and the first thing he was saying before even a hello is "Should I do another *Rush Hour*?"

I was so stunned at his greeting that I answered as sincerely as one could, "I ... don't know."

He went on. "Yeah, I was in Beijing last week. I was walking down the street and I saw Jackie Chan and he said, 'What are you doin' here?' And I said, 'I'm here to see you!' "

Almost as if it were scripted, I swear on all that is holy, I said, "Sounds like the next *Rush Hour* to me." He looked forward and then back to me. "I think you're right!"

Two weeks later the trades announced that they were indeed going to film another *Rush Hour* film for the franchise. I'm not gonna lie, I like to think my little convo with Chris played a part. I don't think an associate producer title is out of the question.

With Chris Tucker. And also this is the fattest I've ever been in my life.

Five Star

College football is hands-down my favorite sport. It's not even close. Sometimes when you say that people immediately jump to "What about the NFL?" And I always respond, "What about it?"

They're different sports.

Yes, the best players in the world do play in the NFL. They're professionals. But the sport of college football is, in my opinion, a far more exciting one.

Some of my friends hear that and lose their minds. They are mostly from the northeastern United States. I point this out for a reason. The majority of their college teams are dog shit. Philly? New York? Boston area? Yeah, I understand why you're not into and don't "get" the appeal of college ball. You have Rutgers, Army (geographically close), and some Ivy League teams. And yes, once every few decades they'll have a decent team. That's nice. Once every few years I take a solid shit, so we can both be proud.

The Midwest, West Coast, and especially the South have another thing happening. It's a culture, an obsessive one. Nothing, in my opinion, compares to college football in the southern United

States. It's not only a religion, it's the most important religion. More important than Christianity? Jesus fuckin' Christ, yes! Of course, it's easy to make the observation that many of these places do not have an NFL team, so college football is all they've got, but honestly, I don't think they even want one.

College games are electrifying, and let's be real, the players are all trying to make it to the NFL. They all want to be twenty-two-year-old millionaires. They play the game *lights out* every week in the hope of getting noticed by the pro scouts. These are the best players in the country, and they seem to be cut from a different cloth than most men. From the time they were in high school, their bigger frames and notable athletic ability set them apart from us mere mortals. Once they get to college, you're seeing the future stars of the NFL.

It's like seeing a porn star when she's still only a stripper. You were there watching her give lap dances for twenty-five dollars *in person* and now she's doing triple anal and winning awards.

The truth is, although there are 130 D1 teams, there are really only twenty-five that matter. The top twenty-five are where you want to be as a team, and they're what most college football fans pay attention to. If you want to get really granular, you can say that what really matters is the top ten, because those are the teams competing for the national championship. Those are the *best of the best*. Everyone who coaches, plays, and watches knows that there is a difference watching *those* teams play. Mall security guards and Secret Service agents both carry badges, but we know who the real deal is. The badasses are the teams you see on Saturday broadcasts in the fall, and those are the schools where I dreamed of playing when I was a kid. I fantasized about playing on prime time at a big-time school: LSU, Clemson, Auburn, Michigan, or my dream team, FSU.

I started playing football in the fourth grade when I was nine years old. My dad *loved* football, and as far back as I can remember he would watch and talk about football almost without pause during the season. Sometimes it was the *only* thing we'd talk about.

He'd lead with "You see the game last night?"

"Yeah. Jerry Rice is unreal!"

"Yeah."

That would sometimes be the entire conversation. My dad, like other dads, had his "go-tos" of complaints when watching games. I can shut my eyes and still hear all of his.

"What a *stupid* penalty. That guy's just stupid."

"This team is *totally* undisciplined."

"Do these guys even practice? They are *terrible*."

Dads love complaining.

I played all through elementary school and middle school, and when I got to be a freshman in high school I thought my dream of playing at the next level was not only reasonable, but probable. After all, I was one of the best players on the freshman team at my big public school in the suburbs of Milwaukee. I had decent size and speed, but more important, I was making plays. I loved playing defense and was regularly in on a bunch of tackles. Now, I should make it clear that my team was *bad*. Beyond bad—like, *really* terrible—but I was a good player on this really shitty team. If I remember correctly, we went 1–9. My dad was so invested in my playing on this epically dreadful team that he delayed our family's move to Florida until late November of my freshman year because he didn't want to disrupt my football season. Seriously. The whole family was ready to move and begin a new chapter of our lives, but my dad told me I couldn't abandon my "platoon," as if we were at war.

When we arrived in Florida, my parents opted to send me and my older sister to a small, private school because they'd heard the large public school was violent.

I don't know how violent that public school was, but the new private school certainly wasn't. It was full of very entitled, wealthy kids who lived in an absurd, protected bubble. All kinds of things I'd never seen before. Kids whose parents were CEOs of major corporations. Kids whose parents would leave them behind while they toured around Europe. I always wondered how those kids managed alone, but when I'd ask them about it, they looked at me like I was barking at them.

"They left money."

"Oh. So you just live alone?"

I could feel their contempt. How could I ask such a silly question?

I started to pay attention to high school football, and it was obvious that they were playing the sport at a different level than my school in Wisconsin. Football in the state of Florida is no joke.

You know how crazy Florida is, right? Insane shit basically is the norm in Florida. Every other news story with an out-of-this-world headline has a good shot of coming out of Florida.

"Man Chews Off Other Man's Face."

"Woman Gets 7th DUI While Shaving Her Pubic Area."

"Magician Zip-tied to Lamppost during Drug Deal Gone Awry."

These are all from Florida, and they are all *real*. I didn't make them up. Do you get it? They're *out* of their fucking minds down there.

Like the rule that you can shoot someone if you *sense* they might hurt you later; they're *that* crazy about football too. There are four states that have elite level high school football: Ohio, California, Texas, and Florida. Many other states love their football too, but those four produce the most top-tier players and often compete to be the best team in the country.

Freshman year in Florida would be my first experience with *spring football*. Every spring the football team practices for roughly three weeks, culminating in a spring game, like an exhibition match. The spring season allows the coaches to see which current freshmen, sophomores, and juniors will be on their team come fall. It's basically a sneak peek. As a freshman I tried out for the football team during the spring, and I was surprised to be named a starter at linebacker for the varsity team. It was wild. I had just turned fifteen, and I was lining up against juniors in high school, two and three years older. And not juniors on a crappy Wisconsin team—these were *Florida* football players. I started thinking that my childhood dreams of playing college ball might become a reality. Those college studs I looked up to must have been named starters on their freshman spring teams too. Also, I knew I was good. I weighed maybe 180 pounds and I could fly around the field. I was aggressive and loved hitting. My coaches were thrilled. They knew they had a player who was hungry, and best of all, I had three full seasons ahead of me. They could mold me into the player I needed to be. And in my eyes, my next-level dream was starting to come together.

That summer my coach approached me about the summer workout schedule. He wanted me there lifting and training, five days a week. It sounded reasonable, but I already had plans.

I think this is the part where someone who really has a dream does the work they're supposed to do. Rocky ran those steps, and Michael Jordan got cut from his JV team and pushed himself, and Buffalo Bill had to follow all those big-boned women home to hone his craft. I should have committed myself to training if college football was really my dream, but my plans, as you now know, involved me spending the majority of my summer in Peru with family. It was something my family did with my mother's siblings and cousins every summer. We'd go down there during our summers, they'd come up here during theirs. When I told my coach, he reacted as you might expect.

"The fuck is in Peru?!"

"My mom's from Peru."

"Oh. She lives down there?"

"No. Coach, I'm going to spend it with my family. I have to."

I mean I guess I didn't *have* to. I could have pleaded with my parents that I *preferred* to pursue my dream, and that dream required me to stay and train. You might wonder how my Marine Corps father didn't push me to stay and work out. There's only one thing he had no power against in this world, and that was my mother. She said I was going down there, and that was that. Part of me wishes that my coach would've forced me to stay, to be the best I could be. But I know deep down I was never going to not go to Peru. I *loved* spending time with my primos and living that Latin life, even as a young teen. Down there you could experience a life that was inconceivable to me here. Late nights, almost every night. Food, dancing, drinking, parties until six in the morning, routinely bribing police officers. I wasn't even sixteen yet! South America and specifically Peruvian culture is one of my favorites in the world. I am the person I am today because of my time there, and I wouldn't trade the experience for anything. I told my coach that my parents wouldn't let me stay, and he asked me to do one thing while I was gone: gain weight.

"Coach, I got you."

Boy, did I.

Before I left, he handed me a large plastic tub of powder. On it, in marker, was written, "Protein & Carbs." It looked like he'd made it at home, all of it. The powder, the jar, the writing.

I left for Lima around 180 pounds. When I returned in August: 210. Yup. A sophomore in high school who looked thirty-five. Yes, he asked me to gain weight. For a two-and-a-half-month stretch he was probably thinking ten or fifteen pounds, not thirty. You could see it in my shoulders and chest, but you could definitely see some of that new weight in my belly too. You know how people in their thirties and forties sometimes say, "My metabolism just changed. I can't eat how I used to." That happened to me at fifteen. My first day at school I saw some jaws drop. That summer I was drinking two of his "homemade" shakes a day and not working out nearly as hard as I should have. I didn't even realize I had gained too much weight until I saw the coach who had given me the powder.

"*Damn,* son. How much did they feed you down there?"

"Not much, Coach. Your shakes did the trick."

"You know you have to *move* and not just drink shakes, right?"

Yeah.

I was still fairly strong, but it was clear that I'd lost a step, so I was moved to play on the line with other fatties.

The next few seasons I played well. I still dreamed of big-time college football, and I especially wanted to be a part of the recruiting process. If you like the NFL, then you are familiar with the draft, where each of the thirty-two teams picks which college player will join its team. It's exciting and, of course, it's a gamble. You don't know how your pick will turn out. It's like Tinder. You can swipe right as much as you like, but until you see her in person you won't know whether she really looks like that or is a black belt in Photoshop. She can say she wants a family, but is she down for anal on the first date? You get the idea. You don't really know what you've got until you try it out.

The college game has something similar to the draft called National Signing Day. This is when the nation's high school players sign letters of intent to play at colleges across the country. Leading up to that day is the recruiting process, where all the college football programs in the country compete for all the talent that's out there. The detail that goes into scouting high school players now is beyond what you can imagine. Players are scouted beginning in middle school if they're good, and college coaches begin sending letters, making phone calls, and even visiting kids in their homes. I wanted to be a part of this, to be courted, wanted. I wanted to be told that my services were deeply desired by all the big schools. This sounded like the closest a young man could get to experiencing what his female counterparts felt all the time: Everybody wants me. Yeah, I wanted my Cinderella moment, is that so crazy? Boys have feelings too.

There's a rating system that is used to rank players coming out of high school. *Rivals*, one of the country's biggest scouting networks, breaks down the star ranking system like this: "A five-star prospect is considered to be one of the nation's top 25–30 players, four-star is a top 250–300 or so player, three stars is a top 750-level player, two stars means the player is a mid-major prospect, and one star means the player is not ranked." Just so you know, yours truly was a four-star player. Pretty cool, huh?

Just kidding. I just felt like writing that because I know some people thought, "Wow, good for him," and those who know definitely shouted, "Bull fuckin' shit!" Those ratings didn't even exist when I was in school.

Rivals.com began in 1998, the year after I graduated. Thankfully, I can't confirm that I would for sure have been a one-star player. At the time, I probably thought I was a three-star because that gave me hope. Looking back, I saw what top-tier looked like, and it wasn't me. They were bigger, faster, stronger. I was above average at best, and that gave me hope. Hope that I'd get the letters, the phone calls, the house calls, and best of all, the recruiting trips. Football prospects are allowed five official visits to major schools when being recruited. These trips are paid for by the schools, and the higher ranked the prospect is, the more bells and whistles come out.

They fly you out, put you up, and then the show begins. Prospects are given a tour of the facilities and often walk out onto the field where they would play with their name on the jumbotron. The game day announcer might even introduce him, so the prospect hears what it would sound like. The recruit is then paired up with a current player, who walks him around campus, showing him the ins and outs and answering any questions the prospect might have. *Then*, the player is wined and dined and *sometimes* there are blow jobs. I'm not saying that any official member of the program is blowing prospective student athletes. I'm saying that a lot of these campuses are filled with young, hot girls who like football players. And hey, they want their school to win too. I know a guy who had a threesome on a recruiting trip. Imagine that. You're in *high school* and colleges want you to attend their school so badly to play a game that two college chicks bang you at the same time.

Add to that the numerous, and I mean *countless* verified reports of players being bribed, and you've got yourself a one-two combo of undeniable fun that I really wanted to be a part of. Play football, get blown, get paid, play more football. Honestly, it sounds like a dream. And it was. A pipe dream.

I got my first recruiting letter late in my junior year. One of the coaches handed me a letter, and in the corner I saw that it was from Holy Cross College, what is known as a Division I-AA school, the second highest tier for athletics. I didn't know what it was at first. When I opened it I realized I was reading my first recruiting letter. *It has begun,* I thought. It was the standard form letter they probably send to hundreds of kids a year: "*We've noticed you are performing well in the classroom and on the gridiron.*" Well, I can tell you right now, they didn't know who they were writing to. I was probably an above-average football player at best, but I was an absolutely terrible student. I mean, truly awful.

I had the second-lowest GPA in my class. Borderline special-needs level. But even as I read that letter, I thought, *This is cool, but I can't wait for the major schools to start sending me stuff.* I knew I wasn't top, top tier, but I thought for sure Indiana, Mississippi State, and Texas Tech would be seeking me out. I mean I didn't *want* to go to those schools, but I would *entertain* their interest. I'd let them fly me out, take me to dinner, put some mid-major mouths on my penis, and at some point I'd have to let them know, "Sorry, but I'm going to be a Seminole/Tiger/Buckeye."

The letters kept coming, but some were from schools I'd never heard of. I got one from Randolph-Macon College. That sounds like some online-only bullshit. I came to find out that this was actually a Division III program, the lowest level of competition. DIII schools do *not* even offer scholarships. So this letter of recruitment was more of a suggestion. "Hey, do you like football? Well, we'll let you pay to play and go to school here."

I was offended.

My best friend and teammate, Steve, got the same letter from Randolph-Macon. Eventually, we decided it'd be fun to go to school and play football together, so we visited the school and met with the coaches. They were thrilled that a couple of big boys like us (each over 240 pounds at the time) would be willing to come to their school and play together. They were not, however, thrilled enough to pay for our trip. There was no free flight, no name on a jumbotron. There was no jumbotron. The "stadium" seated 5,000 people. The big schools have 100,000 seats. They didn't take us to dinner, and there certainly was no blow job offered.

Steve and I actually ended up hiring a stripper from the phone book to come to our hotel room. We paid for it, of course, and it was terrible. She was sad, tired. She ended up drinking with us.

Told us she'd never heard of the college we'd be attending in the fall. It was one mile from the hotel.

When I got back to Florida I let my high school know I'd be attending Randolph-Macon in the fall to play football with my bestie. That summer, almost as soon as high school had ended, I received a phone call from the Randolph-Macon admissions office. There was a problem. My SATs, while not stellar, were acceptable. And my GPA, while deplorable, was also passable, save for one issue. Math. God, I hate math. I didn't always. I was given the "math award" (whatever that is) in the fourth grade, and that led me to believe I had some innate math skills in my brain. But as math progressed I did not. I failed Algebra 1 with a capital F. *FAILED.*

They put me in Algebra 2 even though I clearly wasn't cut out for its easier version. If you didn't guess, I failed that too. Some teachers were perplexed. They looked at me like, "You don't seem this stupid." I'd try to make a case that I wasn't, but then we'd talk about algebra and they'd go, "Wow, he *is.*" Like the opposite of when a child is capable of an adult-level skill.

The admissions office told me that I'd be welcome to go to the school and play football, but I'd have to take a math course over the summer.

"What?"

"Just take a summer school course at the local community college."

"Oh, I don't want to do that."

"Then we can't let you in."

"Okay."

And that was that. All I had to be told was that I needed to take another math class, and the course of my life changed. The problem in retrospect is that I imagined the admissions office would inform the football program that I needed to take a summer school class if I was going to play football there. They didn't.

I told Steve that we wouldn't be going to college together and then scrambled to find a school that would let my dumb ass attend without requiring a summer math class.

I found one. The equally unimpressive-sounding Lenoir-Rhyne College located in Hickory, North Carolina (it has since changed its name to Lenoir-Rhyne *University*). It was literally the only school that accepted me. Talk about low standards. How dumb are the people going there? Apparently about my level of dumb. LRC, as the school is known, has a Division II football program. They didn't recruit me to play, but said I could "walk on," which is another way of saying, "You can try to play here." I was done trying. I was also *very* into smoking weed now, which at the time got a number of players kicked off the team.

August is when football players of all levels—from high school to the pros—report to camp. Players arrive and begin the arduous process of preparing for the season. This begins with what are called "two-a-days," that is, two practices a day in the hottest month of the year. It's brutal. You're going hard, wearing helmets and pads, getting yelled at and running as fast as you can into other people who are running as fast as they can. Once in the morning and again in the afternoon. It's the civilian athlete's version of boot camp. I have to admit it was the only part of football I wasn't going to miss.

I received a call on a Friday in early August. It was the offensive line coach at Randolph-Macon College.

"Segura! We're excited to have you. You all set for Monday?"

"Coach? Monday?"

"Camp starts Monday."

"Coach, I'm not coming to Randolph-Macon."

"What are you talking about? You changed your mind?!"

"No, you guys required me to take a math class."

"A math class?"

"Yeah, Coach. They told me to take a math class and I said no."

"Well, no one told me! Fuck!"

"Sorry, Coach. I thought you would know."

"Well, now I do, and I need a damn offensive lineman!"

Sometimes I can still get lost in the fantasy of "what if?" What if I had stayed and trained instead of gone to Peru? What if I were really committed to that dream? Could I have made it to big-time college ball? Then I think about what those guys really go through, and I remember how much I hate getting up for morning radio to promote stand-up shows. I resent having to wake up at 6:00 a.m. just to sit and talk to people so that I can sell more tickets at my own shows, where I get paid. I was never going to dedicate myself to the grind of playing major college sports. I don't even like morning walks.

West

Vero Beach, Florida, lies in Indian River County. Nationally, there is no county with a greater income disparity gap than this one. That is to say, the wealthiest people who live there earn more—by eye-watering amounts—than the poorest. And they don't even live far from each other. If you start on the east side of the county and head west you can actually see the economic decline. The rich live at the beach, the farthest eastern location you can go, literally right up on the Atlantic Ocean. The beach itself is pristine. Most of the neighborhoods in that area are gated, small shops and boutiques sell everything from flip-flops and sand shovels to designer clothes and handbags. But all you have to do is cross over a bridge, and the view changes.

If you were to go west and a little north you would find yourself in one of the poorest southern areas in the country, all concentrated in a few streets. Homes on cinder blocks with open holes on their sides, taped up with a garbage bag. I had one friend who lived there, and I would drop him off sometimes after football practice. I'd see people sitting on street corners, drinking forty-ounce beers and talking shit. Once, I had dropped my friend off after the sun had begun to set. As I was leaving his neighborhood, I came to a full stop at a stop sign and some teenage kids—the same age as me—*jumped* on the hood of my car! I panicked as they smacked the windshield and shouted. I was terrified before I realized that they were laughing. They were just hazing the white boy. It was sobering, to say the least.

My family lived on the beach, but not in one of the *elite* neighborhoods. It was like we were in the club, but not in the VIP section. West is really where the action lies. The beach side is tame, quiet, reserved, and well, lame. Super lame. Especially if you're young and want...anything to do. It's exactly like a country club if a country club was a whole city. Most of the beach people are old or at least *older*. Nothing really happens there. Golf and cocktail parties are most of it. Everything closes super early. West, on the other hand, is where the regular folks, country bumpkins, and weirdos work and live their lives. So it is the place to go if you're looking for something interesting or fun to happen. Like parties in the orange groves with fire pits and rednecks fighting over whose truck has bigger tires. There were some wealthier people who lived out west as well, probably because you could get so much land. I once dated a girl whose family could have lived anywhere in the world, and they chose to live there.

Once, when I was in my early twenties, I was home for the holidays, and my younger sister, Jane, asked if I would go with her to visit my ex-girlfriend's family on a Saturday night. Our families had been close in the past, but it had been a few years since I'd seen my ex or anyone in her household. Even though there were no hard feelings, I was reluctant.

"Head all the way out west?"

"It's not that bad. Come on."

She was right. It was probably only six or seven miles. The girl and I broke up my sophomore year in college, and I had been out of school a little over a year, a fresh-faced kid living in Los Angeles with showbiz dreams. It might be fun to see them all and share some stories about pursuing comedy in Hollywood. I finished drinking my beer.

"Okay, let's go see them."

My ex had a lot of siblings, and to make things extra weird, Jane had actually dated her younger brother at one point. Yeah, kind of strange, for me at least. They'd remain on again, off again for years. This was probably an on-again phase. Some real Kardashian shit before it was a thing.

As we crossed over the bridge I started complaining.

"This is going to be weird."

"No, it won't. They'd all love to see you."

I went north on Indian River Boulevard.

"What are you doing?"

"Driving."

"They live the other way."

"I can head west on 60 up here."

"That literally makes no sense."

"Let's go home."

"No, it's fine. Fine. Take 60."

I was going the long way because I hadn't driven in Vero for a while, and I had forgotten where to turn. I wasn't only hesitant to go visit the ex's family, I was now being criticized for my driving and directional sense, which is, of course, very threatening to my manhood. I was officially irritated.

"I knew this was a shitty idea."

The road that takes you from IR Boulevard to Route 60 has

a pronounced curve, first to the right, then to the left, before you cross over US 1 and head west on 60. As the road curves right, you notice a large grass field on your left. Now there are businesses there. At the time it was an empty field with a chain-link fence around it.

As we passed the field Jane jumped.

"Did you see that?!"

"See what?" I was already past it.

"I saw something in the field."

"No."

"Go back."

"No."

"Tommy, go back. I saw something out there."

"No."

"Please!"

This was especially annoying because we were on a one-way street, and the only way to see this field again was to navigate a series of turns: left on US 1, left another light up, head *east,* turn back left again on IR Boulevard, before coming back to the street that led to the curve.

"Are you serious? Let's just go see them. I don't want to go back around!"

She pleaded.

"Tommy, I'm begging you. I saw something." I could tell she was sincere. The look in her eyes, her voice. I turned left and complained.

"Goddamnit. Well, what did you see?"

"I don't know ... something."

"Something. Great. Can't wait to see it."

Now as I approached the field again, I slowed down and I saw it too. A light. It was shining from the ground, but not straight up. It was obstructed a bit, but still a notable light in a field that didn't have lights. I parked next to the field, and we got out of my parents' Toyota 4Runner. Jane and I stood next to each other and stared.

"See?"

"Yeah."

I scanned the whole area and then noticed that the fence was missing in a spot. It was torn down.

"Look at that."

It was the point where the curve of the road began. I scanned the field some more and started walking toward the light, and then I saw it. The light was the headlight on a motorcycle. The motorcycle was lying on its side.

"It's a motorcycle."

"Oh my God. Tommy, is there someone there?"

My heart started beating quicker. I walked up to the bike as she stayed by the road.

"No." All I saw was the motorcycle. No one was lying near it.

"Oh my God. Where do you think he went?"

I kept scanning the field. The headlight only lit up portions of it. Then, in a dark spot, I managed to see him.

"Call 911!"

"What?"

"Call 911!"

Twenty yards away I saw a body, and my own body went into fight-or-flight mode. My adrenaline spiked, my throat dried up, I was breathing heavily, and my heart was *racing*. Once I was within a few feet of the body I didn't know what to do. I didn't know what I was going to see. I could only make out that it was a man lying on his side. I didn't know if his face had been torn off or if his insides were splashed all over this field.

"Sir," I was almost whispering. I couldn't get my voice to project.

"Sir!" I was trying.

I inched toward his body for the last few feet, like he was going to jump up and scare the shit out of me with a "Gotcha!"

I extended my index finger and touched his upper arm. "Sir, you... are you... okay?"

He groaned. A deep, short groan. Like when someone is getting you up in the morning and you want to stay in bed because you ate what you were told was a mild edible which turned out to be the corner of a "Star of Death," a 1,000-milligram nightmare treat. The kind that your brain needs days to reboot from.

Back to the scene of the accident:

"He's alive!"

Jane was on the phone in full panic mode.

"He's alive! Come here! Tommy, where are we?!"

I ran back to Jane and took the phone.

"We're between Indian River Boulevard and US 1 heading *west* on 60!" My voice was shivering with anxiety.

I went back to the man with a little more confidence. I have zero medical training, but one thing I've learned over the years from watching a lot of shows with accidents is don't move an injured person. That's pretty universal. A lot can go wrong when you move someone after an accident if you don't know what you're doing. I wasn't even contemplating moving this man, but my thought was to try to *get him* to not move.

"Sir, you've been in an accident. Just stay still. Paramedics are on the way. Just...stay still."

His groan started, and this time it grew, like an engine on an old car. His body started to move.

"Sir, stay still. They're coming."

It was too late. He slowly pushed himself up with his right arm and was sitting up when I saw something that will forever be burned into my memory.

The top of his head flapped open. Like a peel-top can of Sanpellegrino Aranciata. My mouth hung open.

"Oh my God! Sir, don't move!"

He turned his head left and right, and with each movement his head flap followed.

"Oh, fuck!"

Police and paramedics arrived, and then some more and more. I was pacing before Jane called me over to speak to a police officer.

"Can you tell me what happened?"

As I recounted the story of how we found him, a helicopter landed in the field, presumably to take him to the head reattachment center or wherever they specialize in doing what this man desperately needed.

When I finished telling the police officer what happened, he looked at me with a very straight face.

"Have you been drinking?"

"No."

"I can smell it on your breath."

No fucking way. This was going to happen now too? Before I could say anything, he jumped to it.

"You should get out of here. I'd hate for your being a Good Samaritan to end the wrong way."

"Okay."

I got in the car with Jane, and we went west. At my ex's house, what had just happened became the talking point of the evening, obviously. I mean, I was prepared to share tales of open mics where fights break out and commercial auditions where what appear to be mental patients, who are actually actors, pace back and forth in the waiting room as you cross your fingers that Domino's will choose you to introduce their new crustless pizza in a national commercial. But finding an almost dead guy moments earlier seemed like the headline story.

Almost a year later I was living on my own in Hollywood. I lived in an apartment complex on Highland Avenue. All Hollywood apartment buildings have a lobby with locked mailboxes for the tenants. Those mailboxes mean a lot when you're young and trying to make it.

"What's in the mail today?" streams through your mind as you approach your little chamber.

Is it a bill I can't afford? Is it a residual check I wasn't expecting? Maybe it's a card from someone I went to high school with.

On this day I opened my mailbox and saw something unusual. It was a red envelope with big, official-looking lettering and the word "SUBPOENA" clearly printed on it.

I opened it and saw that I was being ordered by a court in Indian River County, Florida, to testify at the trial of a man whose name I didn't recognize. As I read it further it hit me: Motorcycle man was being charged with multiple crimes, and they were ordering me to take the stand. I thought about it. Fly back to Florida to tell this story in court?

I knew better. I should have stayed on the beach that day.

Should have stayed where the little old ladies and the stuck-up retirees go to bed too early and have no fun. I had a traumatic experience and now a potential new world of shit with this trial, all because I agreed to go out west.

Fuck that. I threw the subpoena in the trash.

Lost Wallet

In my heart of hearts I'm a softie, a cuddle bunny. I know I can be grumpy and snarky, but inside every smart-ass is the person they're publicly scared to be. See, I like love stories. I watch *Millionaire Matchmaker* eagerly. My wife was the one who noted how happily I react when couples actually work out. Whereas many watch shows like *Millionaire* to see people clash, I clasped my hands together when it looked like a match had been made, and I would say aloud, "Thank you, Patti," in appreciation of the matchmaker, Patti Stanger. Do I believe in destiny? Fate? You bet. Things happen for *a reason*. You didn't get that job for *a reason*. You broke up for *a reason*. It always works out for the better. I'm an optimist. I like feeling this way. Like, "I met this person because of circumstances—now what?" I always hope that something cool will happen. Maybe this dude owns an island and will invite me and my family to join him for some Sika deer watching. Maybe this lady's dad runs Paramount and I'll be cast in the next funny fat guy thing. Can't wait.

In 2001 I lived in Washington, DC, and was working for *America's Most Wanted* as a "researcher."

Essentially, I would read up on horrific people and pitch doing a segment on one of them to the story editor. It'd go something like this: "I've been reading a lot about this Travis(?) guy. Not a nice fella. He assaulted and killed a bunch of people in Guam and skipped out on bail. We should profile him." It wasn't the most fulfilling job, but at least I was able to pollute my mind with every detail about the lives of the most violent and depraved humans ever.

My time in DC wasn't exactly memorable. I had graduated college and was now fully independent. My first challenge of adulthood was finding a place to live. When I interned at *America's Most Wanted* the summer before, the best part of my time there was due to my housing situation. My uncle and aunt had a place they didn't live at full-time, and they invited me to stay there. It was an incredible place in Georgetown, and I basically had it to myself.

After graduating, I was offered a short contract, but for full employment. At first I was really excited. I mean who wouldn't want to go back and crash at their family's swanky, *way-too-nice-for-me* pad for another few months? I was *set*. But then I called my dad and told him I'd be reaching out to his sister-in-law with the exciting news. He shut that down quickly.

"Can't do that."

"Why not?"

"She already let you live there."

"So, why can't I live there again?"

"You were a college kid. You're on your own now. Also, I'm dropping you from my insurance plan."

"Huh?"

And that was that. Welcome to adulthood. That meant I needed a place I could afford, which meant *not* a place in Georgetown. I mistakenly took up the offer of someone working at *AMW*, who suggested I could move into her house since she was going to be moving elsewhere. I agreed to take it without so much as seeing it. *Big-time rookie mistake.* The house was in College Park, Maryland. Not the worst place, but certainly not that inspiring. I'd be sharing the home with *five* other people I didn't know, and here's the best part: I had a bathroom in my room that other tenants would also use. So when my housemate needed a shit and a shower, he'd tap on my door and get to dumping in my room. Thinking about it is so enraging, I want to go back in time, kill the girl who led me to that shithole of a house, and snap the necks of all my roommates, and then I could be profiled on *AMW* and life would come around full circle.

Socially, I was having a little fun, but I look back now and think I should probably have partied more. What can I say, I was responsible with work and doing what I could with what time I had free. Romantically, it was a roller coaster, but I did manage to go out with a number of women in this short period. I made mistakes. For instance, I went out with two women from work: *huge mistake.* One of them was an executive assistant. She tried to get me to have sex with her behind a curtain at her apartment with her roommate on the other side. I understand that this is completely in line with a lot of people's dreams and fantasies, but all I could picture were our grunts and sounds being unwelcome intrusions on the ears of her roommate, whom I had just met. Call me crazy, but I wanted a *wall.* Even a thin one would do. I know you guys are like, "Come on, Tom. Stop being a bitch. Pound her behind the curtain, bro." Well, I didn't. I like sex to be between me and a woman surrounded by something thicker than a scarf.

She quickly changed her demeanor with me at work, and that should have been a lesson, buuuut . . . then I met an intern. *Oops.*

When you read "intern" you're probably thinking "college girl," and you are correct. But remember, this is me right out of college. Like, I graduated three months earlier. Intern girl was fun and playful, and to her I was a grown man, even though we were extremely close in age. We went on a few dates, and I even stood her up one night, you know, just regular immature, dumb guy stuff. I was young and insecure.

I did get a little action—I slept with my friend's aunt. That wasn't good. She was thirty-two years older than me and looked like Ed Asner in a wig. I had gone to a bar with coworkers who were buying me—a lowly recent graduate—a lot of booze, and so my drinking got out of hand. Later, I would learn that I not only slept with a friend's unfortunate-looking aunt, but I also made out with a lady from accounting while *at* the bar, and yes, she was also *much* older. So I guess I hooked up with *three* women that I worked with, often referred to as the Triple Crown by HR departments. I woke up at Aunt Asner's house and couldn't remember much. I found my clothes on her stairs, and when I went to the kitchen I saw report cards on her fridge. They were from her kids? Her grandkids? All I could think was, *Damn, this bitch is old.* (I mean, I was twenty-two!) Some of the fog of the blackout started to fade, and I was able to recall a few moments from the night before. The memories were followed by intense panic. I had a flashback to kissing her stomach and, as I headed south, her reaching down, grabbing my face, and saying, "You don't want to do that." She warned me like I was about to stick my tongue in the garbage disposal. I guess if I really think about it, it was extremely courteous of her to realize I wasn't going to enjoy doing that.

Kind of like when I signed up to go parasailing in St. Lucia and the guy running the place looked at me and said, "You sure you want to do this? This equipment is old and you're not…small." I mean, now that you say that…no.

I didn't spend all my time going out with women twice my age, but most of my nights were uneventful. Usually, I'd just meet up with some friends in Adams Morgan, drink too much, and go home. Those nights are fun and even *needed* when you're in your early twenties. After a while it hits you. This can't be it, can it? Staying out late with strangers getting hammered leaves you hungover, obviously, but also wanting *more*. I was looking for something, for meaning. I wanted to know and to feel that I had a purpose.

One night led me on an adventure that I was sure was going to change my life on a *Millionaire Matchmaker* twist of fate level. I like to think of it as the "Night of the Lost Wallet." It started when, after a few drinks and striking out at a few bars, I hailed a cab, and something happened that had never happened to me before in my life. A woman asked where I was taking the cab and if I wanted to split it with her.

Is this real life? Am I about to be picked up by an aggressive lady and torn apart back at her place? I hope so. I didn't know much, but I figured I should keep it cool. I looked out the window the way I imagined a *cool guy* would. You know, like the ones in movies who just look completely intriguing staring out a window, brooding over life, their purpose, their desires.

"Is this yours?" she said seductively.

Is what mine? I was sort of hoping she'd be holding one of her breasts as a kinky way of getting things started. Then I could go, "Why, yes, that is mine," and we could put on a show for the driver.

I turned and saw she was holding a wallet. And I went, "No, it's not mine." And she said, "Oh, it must be the previous rider's wallet. I'll just give it to the driver."

I stopped her and said, "Don't do that. Give it to me. I'll get it back to the rightful owner." I know that sounds like something Humphrey Bogart would have said in the 1930s, but I instinctively said it and truly meant it. I imagined this wallet meant something to someone, and my prejudice told me the driver wasn't the kind of guy who'd go out of his way to return it. At that moment I was deciding to take this burden on myself.

My fellow passenger didn't hesitate. She looked at the wallet and handed it right over. Now it was all on me. I needed to find the owner. But, here's the honest-to-god truth: *I really wanted to.* I've had wallet-finding fantasies my whole life. I've seen stories in the news, feel-good pieces where a guy returns a wallet to the owner of a grocery chain. And then the owner tells him, "Wow, that was awfully nice of you. Have you ever been to Monte Carlo? Come spend the summer on my yacht there."

I didn't know what to expect when I opened the wallet, but I wasn't expecting what I found. It had two dollars, a grocery store rewards card, and a community college ID with a photo and a name, Justin. Justin's photo was as ordinary as his name. Just a regular-looking college kid. Everything about it was telling me I should discard it and move on with my life. Why would anyone want this back? Will they not be allowed in the student center for the hypnotist show? Will they no longer get the discount on beer that they most certainly can't afford with two dollars? I realize that most people would end their quest here, and that would be understandable. *I'm not most people,* I told myself. *It's too easy to quit here. This poor guy, whoever he is, needs this back.* I told myself that I had no right to judge the fact that this guy didn't have anything worth a shit in his wallet; it's still his wallet and it's going to pay off.

A minute later we were at my cab companion's stop. She didn't even turn to say good night, she was just gone. But hey, at least I still had this underachiever's wallet on me. At this point I felt like it was a challenge. *I'm a fuckin' researcher at* America's God Damn Most Wanted. *I find international bad guys. I can find this dude.* And I *really* wanted to. I had such hope that it would be inspiring, the kind of story they show you on *Good Morning America.* The feel-good piece that helps offset all the sadness and despair that fill most newscasts. I imagined an anchor telling the viewers that "against all odds and despite the improbable obstacles in his path, Tom Segura knew he had to return this item to its rightful owner." The tone of the piece would be not unlike the stories of World War II vets who promised they'd deliver a message for a fallen brother. I imagined that the recipient of this item, Justin, would not only be grateful, but curious. Curious about me, and from that a lifelong friendship would be born. Perhaps a business where we'd both thrive. Certainly, family vacations where the two of us would take turns picking destinations and bringing our families with us. It was going to be amazing!

When I got home, I laid out his items and grabbed a notepad and a pen. My plan was to document all my clues and methodically piece this mystery together. I knew it was going to take real work, but I was prepared and inspired by the homicide investigators I'd seen on TV over the years. They didn't give up on solving their cases, and I wasn't going to give up on mine. My first move was to call the grocery store. Looking back, it is laughably, hysterically stupid to think that a grocery store would help you find someone.

"Thank you for calling Publix."

"Yeah, I'm trying to find someone I've never met. Do you think you can help me?"

"Are they here in the store?"

"No, somewhere in the greater metro area."

"Would you like to speak with someone in the meat department?"

"Why not?"

You've been to grocery stores before, right? Not to be rude, but the vibe in most grocery stores in my experience isn't one of "let's get our forensics team on this." It's usually more of a "we are willing to overlook felonies if you know how to stock a shelf."

I was shot down immediately. The person on the phone didn't even entertain the idea that they could help me find the owner of the wallet.

"Yeah, I don't know."

Hung up.

My detective instincts perked up. I had my best information right in front of me and I hadn't yet used it. Mr. Lost Wallet, aka Justin, had a community college ID. I thought it could be wrapped up quickly. I'd call the school, tell them to tell the student I had his lost property, and that'd be it. After a few hours of talking to different departments, I learned that our man was no longer a student. When I asked for contact info, they said, "We have a number." *Bingo!* I was getting warm and it felt good!

I called the number and instead of hearing "Hello" I was

greeted by what can only be described as the grunt of a man who was shitting and wished he hadn't answered the phone.

"*Yeah?*"

"Hi." I explained to the man, who was presumably grinding out a rugby football–sized turd as he listened on the phone, that I had found this wallet in a cab, pulled out this one identifying card, and the school had directed me to this number. I then asked, "Are you...Justin?"

"He's my son."

Oh, great, I'm thinking. I've solved the case. Yes, I was inconvenienced by having to make *two* whole phone calls for my investigation, but still, totally worth it. This man is getting his wallet back. But then...

"He's a real asshole."

Huh?

"Who is?"

"Justin, my son."

"Oh, well, I just want to return his property."

But the man, Justin's father, wasn't as interested in my quest as I was.

"He never finishes anything he sets out to do. He's a loser, and I don't think he's going to amount to shit."

And then he hung up the phone. If I hadn't experienced that call myself, I'd be hard-pressed to believe it. I actually found the parent of the man whose wallet I had in my possession, and the parent not only went out of his way to not accept the property, but also to insult his own son in spectacular fashion.

This felt like an episode of *Black Mirror*. Was Justin's father going to lure me into his life and turn me into the son he never supported only to verbally abuse me in the way I suspect he must have tormented Justin?

I shared the story with a few friends, who were mostly incredulous at the man's behavior. After a while I had to move on. I wasn't going to be spending any more time trying to get this wallet back to Justin. I had exhausted every reasonable course of action to return someone their two dollars and their discount card for eggs.

A few months later, my cousin Jeannette was visiting town, and we decided to meet up for lunch. We chose a casual eatery in Georgetown, nothing fancy. After we sat down and exchanged a few pleasantries, the server approached our table. He asked whether or not we wanted something to drink. I looked up at him and blurted out, "Justin!"

Confusion immediately crept onto his face. "How do you know my name?"

"Dude, I have your wallet!"

I was glowing, almost hyperventilating.

Do you know what Justin's response was?

"Cool. Do you have it on you?"

First of all, no. I'm not walking around with a second wallet at all times, asshole. Secondly, isn't anyone at least a little impressed that I've stared at this man's community college photo for so long that it's burned into my head and two seconds after seeing him for the first time I'm able to make a positive ID? Even looking back on that now, I think that's remarkable. I think it's one of the most spectacular, improbable, outrageous moments of my or anyone's life.

Justin was ready to move on.

"Can I get you guys something to drink?"

Justin might have been calm, but I was truly speechless. I felt destiny had connected us in that moment. It was the only explanation. Why else would I have spent the time and energy to return this man's nearly worthless possession if I wasn't at least going to get to know him? I spent the remainder of that lunch going into every detail with my cousin. She didn't believe me at first, and who could blame her? But as the story unraveled she became enraptured.

"You've *never* met him?"

"No."

"Tommy, this is so weird. It's fate. Are you going to marry him?"

"Maybe. Maybe this is a sign I should try something really gay with someone."

After I paid the check, I approached Justin.

"Hey, man, so how should I get it to you?"

"Get what?"

"The Mona Lisa."

He just stared at me. Which, I guess, is fair. I had made a joke because I thought it was obvious what I wanted to *get to him*. I didn't just want to return his property, I wanted to hang out. Something was supposed to happen. I believed it. I imagined we were going to hang out and, I don't know, open a juice bar or build a cabin in the woods or measure each other's dicks, but I didn't want to scare him, so I played it cool.

"I was kidding. I could return your wallet to you."

"Okay."

At this point I told myself, *He must be shy*. Of course I wanted more out of him, but he's just reserved.

I had recently moved out of the apartment I was living in, so I was staying in a hotel for a few days. I told Justin to meet me there so I could return his wallet. Looking back, it was a little surprising that he had zero apprehension, but then again, he had displayed absolutely no emotion thus far. *I'm* the one who should have insisted on meeting his cold, lifeless eyes in a public place.

I got increasingly nervous as the meeting time we had agreed upon approached. I think I was expecting him to transform into another person. I told myself he was simply being professional at work, and now with the chains of employment no longer binding him, he could let loose and be the guy I knew he was capable of being. In my mind I was going to open my hotel room door and before I could even say hello he would throw his arms around me. Perhaps he would present me with a gift that he had brought as a small tribute. He would go on to acknowledge everything I had done and explain what it all meant to him. Then our new life would begin. Justin and me, the two greatest friends ever.

My reverie was interrupted by a knock at the door. My heart started to race. *This was the moment.* If this was being scored like a movie, the music would start to swell here. The violins, the cellos would be building up to the climactic moment.

I opened the door. Justin stood in front of me. I held my breath for a beat. I was a little surprised to see his face still conveyed zero emotion.

"Here's your wallet."

I handed it over.

"Thanks."

He turned and walked toward the elevator. I watched him press the call button. He didn't say another word or even look back at me.

I shut the door and sat on the bed, contemplating what an extraordinarily disappointing interaction I had just experienced.

I wanted so much more. This was supposed to be the magical moment that made me feel connected to humanity. The moment where I stopped laughing at people who did yoga and meditated and lit candles as they chanted. This would erase my cynicism and make me one of them. A loving hippie dippy. The kind I always mocked and dreamed of assaulting.

Then it hit me all at once. *Justin's dad was right*. Justin is a piece of shit! It turns out this *was a life-changing moment. I was* enlightened by the lost wallet experience. I'd learned something they don't teach you in school: The world is full of disappointment. In sports, jobs, but most of all, in people.

The encounter with Justin could have been awesome. I wasn't crazy to want it to be. *There are* people out there who would have reacted the way I wanted him to. But of course not *everyone* can be what you want them to be. That day I realized that there are two types of people in the world: people who would have shit their pants when a stranger called them out by name because the stranger had found their lost wallet and people like Justin. Detached, uninteresting, coasting through life. The world has a bunch of Justins in it, and they are to be avoided.

It's like I was watching myself on a bizarro episode of *Millionaire*, and even though it wasn't one of the happy, fulfilling matches that make me celebrate, the lesson was big enough to make me clasp my hands and say, "Thank you, Patti. Thank you."

Jill Scott

American 614, LAX to BNA, 11:22 a.m.

Asking celebs for photos is a big no-no. I mean, *sort of*. Obviously, they are famous and obviously they are aware that they have fans and those fans would like to take a picture with them. There are certain situations where taking a photo with a celeb is normal, even encouraged, like at a meet-and-greet or a celebrity outing: a golf tournament fund-raiser, for instance. Famous people get hit up for photos constantly, and they each handle it however they choose to. But there are also times when you're definitely not supposed to ask a celebrity for a photo, and one of those times is when you are actually hanging out with them. If you're at a party or a dinner or, I don't know, sitting next to one on a flight, they're supposed to be able to let their guard down and just talk to you like a regular person. I get that. But I can be weak. Not long ago I was invited to do a big fund-raising show at Madison Square Garden with Pete Davidson. He put together a show where the proceeds would go to charities that benefit victims of the 9/11 terrorist attacks and their families. The lineup was incredible: Dave Chappelle, Jon Stewart,

Chris Rock, John Mulaney, and a dozen more comedy stars plus yours truly. It was an absolute honor to perform on the show. When my best friend from high school, Steve, saw the announced lineup, he told me he'd be flying from Florida to New York City because he had to see it. Steve has always loved getting "hooked up" with free stuff. In high school he'd ask the girl working at McDonald's to give him free fries. He'd always angle for an extra set of anything he was buying: socks, oil, iced tea. He lives to see how much *pull* you have that can benefit him. I knew he'd flip at this event. I got him tickets and a backstage pass and then unleashed him. It was hilarious.

"Is it cool if I ask Jon Stewart for a picture?"

"I wouldn't. I mean he's just hanging out."

"Okay . . . Hey, Jon, can I get a picture?"

I cringed.

He then did the ultimate faux pas after asking a celeb for a

Jon Stewart, me, and Steve, courtesy of Ansel Adams.

photo; he literally couldn't figure out his phone. It kept facing the wrong way, wasn't taking a photo when he pressed the button, and Jon stood there like a champ. He waited and waited. Steve, clearly nervous, was fumbling his phone like a clumsy bear. Jon waited some more, and the best Steve got was this: a blurry, moving photo.

From there we went to Chappelle's after-party. As you can imagine, more celebrities were casually enjoying themselves at a party where it was announced *not* to pull out your phone. Chappelle literally got on a mic and said, "We don't take pictures here. We make memories."

Moments later, high school Steve had his phone in hand.

"That's Pete Davidson!"

"Yeah."

"Is it cool?"

"I mean, I wouldn't."

"Hey, Pete! Can we?"

Pete was ear-to-ear smiling and obliged.

I turned to Steve. "Fuck it. Ask whoever you want." And I took the photo.

Pete Davidson and big, dumb Steve.

Next was Jon Hamm, then Q-Tip, and on and on. It wasn't until months later, when I was revisiting chapters in this book, that I realized I'm just like Steve. If you're someone I *want* a pic with, I'm not going to hold back.

Jill Scott hates salmon. There it is. There's all the proof you need that my conversation with her really happened.

We flew from Los Angeles to Nashville and talked for a lot of the flight. I recognized her, but I didn't let her know immediately. We were in first class, and when the flight attendant came by, one of the options for the meal was salmon. Now, I'm not insane. I don't get salmon on planes, but when you're down on Earth, like walking around with your feet on the ground, and there's a body of water nearby, salmon is one of my favorite things to eat. I love salmon, and I told Jill Scott that.

I said, "Salmon's amazing," and she goes, "I never eat salmon."

"Well, how are you having it prepared?"

"In no way. I just do not eat salmon."

So I started to describe my favorite way to prepare salmon, which is a classic French technique: Skin on one side of the filet. You put the skin side down in a pan with a lot of butter, some might say *an obscene* amount of butter, to which I say, "No such thing." You season your salmon with salt and pepper and place it in the skillet on a low-medium heat. And then, after a few minutes, you flip it over. You want high-quality salmon, obviously, and it should be cooked medium rare. To achieve this, cook the skin side down for five to six minutes, then flip it and cook for another three minutes. Now, to feel like a chef, you can tilt the pan and with a spoon gather the butter that is forming a pool into that spoon and pour it back onto your filet. If you want to go all the way Français, then you're going to need to make some beurre blanc sauce, but even without it, this is one of Tommy's go-tos and it's delicious. I told her all of this, and she actually seemed intrigued. "Okay, I think I'll try that."

Did I just get *Miss Jill Scott* to try salmon?

I asked her how she was liking Nashville and if people were friendly. And she said, and I quote, "I don't need them to be friendly. Just cordial and polite is enough."

I nodded in agreement, knowing exactly what she meant. "Friendly" can be *a lot*. Especially when it's not real. When it's not real, you know it, and it feels gross, like when a salesperson keeps laughing as they make meaningless small talk.

"You know, it's fall so it's not hot, but it's not cold either! Hahahaha!"

It's phony.

And then, as the flight was ending and we were pulling up to the gate, I said, "Do you mind if I get a picture with you?" And she said, "Wow, you're better at this than I am." And I snapped one.

Oddly enough, it's one of the only pictures I can't find.

Update: I ran into Jill Scott last night in Nashville. I told her we flew together a few years back and went into the details of the

above story, and she said, "I don't like salmon. I don't fuck with anything pink." I asked her for a pic, exactly the way you're not supposed to. Here it is.

Second update: I found the original photo too.

A Lot Too Much

I never imagined I'd be one with any drug stories. In elementary school I was so clean-cut my hair was parted and combed like a good boy. I just wanted my parents to be happy with me and to continue saying what a sweet kid I was. I didn't even curse until seventh grade. One time my neighbor Dan and his brother Jimmy across the street grew so fed up with my reluctance to curse that they put me in a headlock and pulled out a knife.

Dan told Jimmy, "Cut him if he doesn't say 'Fuck.'"

I wouldn't do it.

Under the threat of permanent and perhaps fatal injury I refused to say something unbecoming of a fine young boy. Fast-forward thirty years and I'm Mister Fuck-Fuck. Fuckin' you right up your shit-shoot, fuck face. I just don't give a fuck. I don't know when I changed, but it was a slow process of trying things that were *fun*.

Drugs were something I associated with losers. People you saw strung out on the streets, those were people who did drugs. I didn't realize that those were just people who did *too many* drugs. Drugs, like anything else, can be a lot of fun if you consume them in moderation. When you take the right amount of drugs it's great 'cause you're chillin' and you're cool and you know you're the best.

My older sister first introduced me to drugs. And that's a stretch of a statement because what she introduced me to was weed. I hit the pipe and then I had a heart attack and was rushed to the emergency room. Ha! Of course that didn't happen (but more on that later). No, I got moderately high and thought, *Okay.*

Later I would do whippits and smoke a lot more weed at UW Madison. I wasn't enrolled there. I was fourteen and visiting my friend's brother, who left a bunch of shit on his coffee table, and since he left us alone in his place we finished all his drugs for him. I pretty much stuck to weed after that, mostly on the weekends, but my senior year in high school I decided to up the ante. First it was ecstasy. Today the kids call her Molly, but back in the nineties it was simply "X." It was supposed to make you feel like you were jizzing out of all your pores and you were going to be rock hard. At least that's what I was told. I think I must have had a placebo pill because I just *acted* like that was happening to me, minus the hard-on. I didn't really fall in love with a drug until I tried GHB.

I was led to believe that bodybuilders were taking it after workouts by a classmate who had a ridiculous physique for a sixteen-year-old. I mean this kid had the kind of size and definition you see on a dedicated adult bodybuilder. My desire to be ripped without working out and dieting made it a perfect match for me. The street version of GHB was sold at that time in twenty-ounce water bottles, the kind you've probably drunk from for years. These bottles were filled with a liquid that at a glance might make you think it was just water. A closer look would reveal what was inside was yellowish in hue and tasted *just* like ocean water. To give you an idea of the potency of the GHB we were taking at the time, a "hit" would be one bottle cap. The bottle cap on a bottle of water is all you needed to get absolutely *lit*. How much fluid does it take to fill up *the cap* of a water bottle? Six *droplets*? Ten? This shit was straight *gas*, homie.

After you were able to get past the horrific taste, you were about thirty seconds from euphoria. We used to call it "Perma Grin." I had never done any other hard drugs, but this felt the way those drugs were portrayed. In movies they always show someone shooting up heroin and then lying back as their eyes roll into the back of their heads. GHB did that to me. I didn't always pass out, but I always felt good. Someone could spit in my face and my response would be, "Maybe he thought I was thirsty." I finally found a drug I could really throw my weight behind.

We were so cocky my senior year of high school, in the way only seniors in high school can be, that we began doing "hits" of GHB during our lunch break, a free period where we were permitted to leave campus, and returned for the remainder of the school day out-of-our-minds high. The arrogance in retrospect was astounding. I remember Craig, the kid who introduced me to "G," was particularly brazen with it. We had just stuffed our faces with Miami Subs when he did a quick hit. He casually asked me if I wanted one too.

My nerves took over.

"Before we go back?" We still had three periods left! I mean, I was still transitioning from the good boy who parted his hair to *this* guy who was doing drugs!

"Who's gonna know?"

Welp! That's all it took. I was *convinced*!

No one ever suspected a thing. GHB didn't make your eyes red the way weed did, and it didn't impede your ability to listen or follow instructions the way alcohol would. You just felt great and no one knew it. I did have a fair warning scare once, but I was too young and too dumb to pay attention to it. I went to a Clint Black concert with friends and did some hits throughout the night, but on the way home a couple of us blacked out. When we woke up we realized we had lost a lot of time. We had no sense of what we had seen or done or how much time had gone by (it was about two and a half hours). We were used to the idea of alcohol blackouts. While scary, they make sense. They usually happen because you went overboard with liquor. You can only blame yourself because the warning is explicit: *Thirty-two ounces of Everclear and Gatorade is going to end poorly.*

But we hadn't had any alcohol, just a handful of sips of some *Georgia Home Boy*, like we usually do over the course of a night. The blackout scared us. Not enough to quit, of course. Just enough to not do any more that night.

When I went to Lenoir-Rhyne University a few months later I brought a full twenty-ounce bottle of GHB with me. This would typically last me two and a half months. I didn't account for my tolerance increase and, more importantly, my sadness. I was depressed and getting more so as reality set in. I was leaving what I knew, and instead of the big campus college I had dreamed of going to, I was in a sleepy country town in the foothills of the Appalachian mountains. During the ten-hour drive to campus, I sat in the back of my parents' SUV, fumbled through my bag, and snuck shots whenever they were distracted, which was pretty much the whole time. I was high for the majority of the drive, and as soon as they waved goodbye at dropoff, I took another hit. Clearly, I was looking for an escape, and my water bottle was all I needed.

My first memory of being *at* college as a brand-new, first-year student was going to my dorm room and hearing that there was a freshman orientation in the auditorium. We were required to attend. I skipped and got high alone in my room.

If I'm being honest, I was lonely, insecure, and slightly depressed. I didn't want to be in this hillbilly town in North Carolina, but I didn't see any other options. College was mandatory in my family. It wasn't even plausible that someone would bring up *not* going to college. I had fantasies of being a filmmaker at the time, and I thought comedy would be my route. I never applied to a proper film school. I was too intimidated given that mediocre schools were already turning me down because of my horrendous high school GPA, and I was holding on to the idea of playing football. I rationalized that I would get into a communications program, and they have radio, print, and *video* specialties. Video isn't film, but at least it's making something you can show people. I went to LRC because it was literally the only school that accepted me.

My first few weeks at school I was getting high constantly and doing so in secret from my roommate. I was doing it so much that my stash soon ran out, and now I was looking for my favorite drug in a new town. And trying to find GHB, if you haven't guessed, isn't like trying to find weed. Most people had no idea what you were asking for, but as luck would have it, one guy did. He was a sixth-year senior, a dumb-dumb. I first encountered him when I was looking for weed. I was told he was someone to ask, but he had a lot of questions for me.

"You're a freshman?"

"Yeah."

"Where you from?"

"Florida."

"Florida, huh? What brought you here?"

"School. We both go to school here."

It didn't take me long to realize that he and a few others I'd met were hesitant to sell to me because of my physical appearance. Not that I'm particularly intimidating, but I did look... older. In my circle of friends I've been called the "Albert Pujols of Comedy." This is a reference to the regular practice of Dominican baseball prospects doctoring their birth certificates to appear younger than their real age. At seventeen I was buying booze without a fake ID. Not only did the cashiers not even ask for ID, but they also called me "sir." *Sir.* People guessed I was in my late twenties. The trend continues to this day. As I'm writing this I'm forty-two, but I'm often told, "I thought you were in your fifties."

How flattering.

A big part of it then and now is the beard. It's an age enhancer, and as the grays settle in, the age people guess goes up. I started shaving when I was fourteen, and I could grow decent stubble at seventeen. I did it then because I could. It was a subtle reminder to my less hairy friends, "I'm *definitely* more of a man than you."

When the drug dealer had me asking him for an unusual, difficult-to-find liquid downer he was majorly suspicious, thinking I might be a narc, but he agreed to get hold of some, and I was thrilled.

He demanded that we do the deal in the entryway of one of the dorms—it was clear he wanted to control the environment. When I arrived he was waiting on the opposite end of the hall, about thirty feet away, staring at me like we were about to pull pistols in a duel. I knew he was wondering if I was a cop, and I didn't know how to convince him I wasn't. As I walked toward him he put one hand up, signaling me to *stop*. He looked around as if at any moment my backup was going to kick open the doors behind me, guns drawn, and holler at him to get his *FUCKIN' FACE ON THE GROUND!* I just stared back with my blank face and gestured, "What now?" He gave the universal single hand gesture for "Where's the cash?" The whole thing felt like charades for entry-level drug dealers. I held up the money, and he pointed at a pay phone. As I walked over to place the cash down, I saw the bottle. *YES, DUDE!* I was so excited to have my old friend back. I put the money where he'd pointed and hauled ass back to my room, ready to get down with ocean water sips and perma smiles.

What I had in my hand, though, was a *far* inferior product. It was GHB *Light*. Them Florida boys had the ill shit, and these Carolina crackers had some heavily diluted, weak bullshit. The Carolina stuff wasn't the right color. It was more clear, the taste was not as sharp, and the effect was lame. What was I going to do? I doubled up on shots and got as high as I could. It was a serious letdown. Eventually I stopped buying it because the Carolina product wasn't worth the hassle. I'd rather just smoke a bunch of weed.

It wasn't that big of a sacrifice. I was smoking weed nightly with some new friends in the dorm and enjoying the hell out of it. It was the first time away from home for all of us and we bonded with one another over what we loved: weed, music, and laughing. We'd hit the bong, listen to hip-hop, and play Madden until the sun rose. It actually hit me by surprise when it was time to go home for Thanksgiving break. That's when I remembered I could get some of the good stuff again. My first time home as a college student now had a purpose. I wouldn't just be seeing my family and hanging with high school friends, I'd have a real opportunity to load up on some *Go Hard Boss* sauce and bring it back to college.

The way it worked in Vero Beach, Florida, the day after Thanksgiving was the big day to party.

That Friday I met up with a huge group of high school friends and found *the* guy who always had the good stuff back in high school. I was ready to get ripped on my favorite three-letter combo. He told me he'd have some *later*, but that I might not even want it because he had gotten ahold of some primo ecstasy from Miami. I was hesitant because I was sure of what the GHB would do to me and I had a prior experience with "X" that was disappointing, but my dealer said this was different and that I wouldn't be let down by *these* pills.

"Just get me the 'G,' dude."

"Later. I'll have some later, but this shit is killer. Newest shit from the 305."

It sounded like I would *have* to wait, and this was the only other thing he had, so I gave him cash, ate the pill, and within a few minutes I was…disappointed. I didn't feel anything. I ran over to him. "Hey, man. I don't feel shit."

"Uh, you *just* took it. Give it thirty minutes."

Fuck. Thirty minutes? See, that was the beauty of the liquid stuff. You barely waited thirty *seconds*.

But I thought, *Okay, in thirty minutes I'm gonna be coming out of every pore.* Forty-five minutes later, nothing. And worse, I couldn't find my dealer. I wanted to feel something *now*. I did what I had the easiest access to—a drink, then another.

About thirty minutes later there was a company move. Everyone was heading over to Bobby's, a well-known bar on the beach. As soon as I got there I had a couple screwdrivers. I was on my way to getting fucked up, but it was *drunk* fucked up, not the high kind that I craved.

I just kept drinking.

As I was on my way back to the bar I spotted him, my former classmate/current drug supplier. I was elated. He saw the look on my face and right away he knew what I wanted, a swig of that salty water.

"All right, come on, Tom."

"Dude, I never felt that ecstasy."

"Really?"

What I was definitely feeling were those screwdrivers. By this time I had lost count, but it could've easily been a dozen. I was drunk.

We went out to his car, and I sat in the passenger seat. He pointed at the ground between my legs, and there it was, something I had never seen before; a one-gallon jug of GHB. Quick reminder: I had only had standard twenty-ounce water bottles full of the stuff, which is how the dealers distribute it to consumers. This jug was predistribution. A gallon wasn't only astonishing in volume, but also unorthodox. How am I supposed to take a hit? You can't pour it into the cap on a gallon jug.

"Take a swig."

I picked up a full, one-gallon jug of GHB and held it up to my lips. *How much do I sip? What's a bottle cap worth? How many screwdrivers have I had?*

A moment later, my mouth was full. *Full* of GHB. I had tipped back way too much. I knew it was too much. My first thought was, *You can't spit it out. It's drugs. It's valuable.*

I hesitated for a second then swallowed. Whoa. *How much did I just take? That was way more than a water bottle cap. Five? Seven?*

I put the jug down, thanked him, and I was ready to rock. I went straight to the bar for a couple more screwdrivers. I was dancing, high-fiving, and just generally having a helluva time. I sat down for a break and it hit me, I was FUUUUUUUCKED UP! Oh well, who cares. I'm chillin' with a girl on my lap and people all around. That was it. My last memory of the evening.

I woke up eight hours later staring at fluorescent lights. I was restrained. I couldn't sit up and I couldn't move my arms. For a brief moment I felt absolute terror. A woman I recognized leaned over me. She was a classmate's mother, a doctor. "Tommy, you overdosed. You're in intensive care at the hospital."

Fuck. How is this real?

I closed my eyes and wished as hard as I could, not that I would recover, but that my parents wouldn't find out. Then I opened my eyes and there they were, looking at me. I'll never forget that look. I killed a part of them that day.

Next, the nurses put a pen in my right hand, the hand I do *not* write with. They held out a pad of paper and told me they needed to know what happened so they could treat me accordingly. I already had tubes in my nose and others going down my throat. They were pumping my stomach full of liquid charcoal so the chemicals in whatever I took would come together and a forced regurgitation would take place. Before I could explain what happened I had to deal with my parents, the look on their faces. I scribbled on the pad, "Are you mad at me?" They both shook their heads, and my dad added, "We're not mad at you, Tommy. Just disappointed."

Hey, thanks, dude. Think you could have skipped saying that since I'm, you know, coming out of a coma. No? Okay, cool.

Next the doctors pressed me, "What did you take? We need to know what's in you."

I jotted down "Heroin." Everyone's eyes bugged out. You could hear the air conditioning coming through the vent and after a beat I wrote, "Kidding." Not a lot of laughs, but it made me feel better.

I spent two more days puking in the ICU. Every blood vessel in the whites of my eyes ruptured. I looked like I had gone up to Cain Velasquez and told him his mother was a cunt. After yet another day I was finally in a normal recovery room when the doctor who saved me, the one who was able to fit a breathing tube down my throat when no one else could, came to visit. He told me he had never seen a toxicology report like mine where the patient ended up alive.

It turns out I had basically everything in me: barbiturates, amphetamines, cocaine. I didn't understand. I didn't take those things. "The drugs you thought you were taking were spiked. They were just cocktails of other drugs. Happens a lot. I just can't believe you're still here."

I thought about it. How *did* I survive? Don't give me that miracle shit. There has to be a real-world reason. I asked him why he thought I made it through. He looked at the chart and then to me.

"You're two hundred fifty pounds. That's a lot. Sometimes it's good to be fat."

Concha Mi Madre

My mother has a very direct way of speaking. She doesn't have the ability to bite her tongue.

When my father's brother was moments from remarrying after his thirty-six-year marriage ended, my mother called my father and insisted that she speak to him since she wasn't able to attend. My uncle no doubt thought he was going to hear "Congratulations!" or well-wishing of some kind. Instead, my mother told him that she was sorry to say it, but she thought he was making a huge mistake. He shouldn't marry the woman he was mere moments from exchanging vows with.

I can't imagine saying that to someone. I can't imagine what it must be like to hear that when you're literally minutes from tying the knot. But I can imagine my mother doing that, not only because I was at the wedding staring at my uncle as he took the call, but because my whole life my mom has said whatever is on her mind to me and everyone else.

Her justification for being so direct is that she can't "not be herself." I think the rest of us would be thrilled if sometimes she could stop being herself and become someone else entirely. She tells you exactly what she thinks about the way you look, what you're wearing, what you're doing in life, who you're dating, how you should feel, your opinions, thoughts, career, and what you should buy her.

Literally today, the day I am writing this, she called to tell me that there weren't any cars that she could *find* locally to purchase. That is, of course, not true. There are a dozen dealerships less than three miles from where she lives. If you understand my mother you'd know that this translates to, "Will you buy me a car?" My reply was, "Keep looking. I'm sure you'll find one."

My favorite asshole move of hers is when she tells you *not* to be upset about something. Maybe the dog jumped on your back and scratched you, or you just found out you didn't get the job you wanted. She has this really spectacular talent for waiting until the exact worst moment, down to the second, when you're completely frustrated, before she drops the always helpful, "Don't be upset."

It's pretty cool!

If that's a lot to take in, imagine if I were describing your goddamn mother, because that is mine. She is a tornado of tumultuous emotions wrapped in a petite Latina woman's body.

She'll look you dead in your eyes and tell you, "You don't look good" while she's wearing thirty-five-year-old pajamas and her hair looks like it has been set on fire. She'll tell you that you're wasting your money on something you want to indulge in for yourself, but she will follow that up by telling you that she "needs" the new iPhone. My favorite of her hilarious hypocrisies is her guidance on health and wellness. She will lecture anyone within earshot about what they should be doing to achieve optimum human performance. She will display a face of horror while you eat something that she finds unappetizing or unhealthy.

"How many pieces of bacon are you going to have? My god, you're going to turn into a pig."

"It's only two pieces of bacon."

"Yeah, but look how big they are. Those two pieces might as well be six pieces."

That's probably the nicest exchange you can have with her about what you're eating. A lot of times it's much more dramatic. *Cringe face* followed by "Ugh, what is that? Yuck! You're eating fish in a disgusting sauce? I want to vomit."

Such a fun way to enjoy your meal, right? You're just eating dinner and the commentary is free. Then there are her exercise opinions.

"You need to run and do some weights. Right now it's too hot. Wait until after dinner."

I should point out that she is small, five foot five, and maybe 110 pounds. You might be thinking, *Wow, so she's really healthy and just sharing her insights?* Not exactly.

My mom eats like a toddler. I don't mean that she eats exactly what a toddler eats. What I mean is that she eats what a toddler *wishes* they could eat all day. My mother begins her day by having two pieces of toast covered in butter and a super-rich jam of some kind. Apricot and strawberry jams have been a fixture in her diet for decades. That toast can hold her over for hours. She often skips lunch, but she doesn't skip snacks. She likes pastries like prune bear claws, cookies, and a sweet Italian bread called panettone. These are the foods that fuel her midday. Once those nutrients are done being absorbed by her desperate muscles, it's on to dinner. Here is where nine times out of ten her desired meal is chicken tenders, a small serving of rice, and French fries. I've seen her request this at Michelin-starred restaurants.

"Mom, this is one of the best restaurants in the world. Don't you want to try their signature dish?"

"I want fries."

Cheap date, sure, but how can you pass on this world-class food? For her this isn't even a consideration.

As I mentioned before, she can be a *real* asshole. It's actually impressive. She'll ask if you're dumb because you said something or did something that she simply doesn't agree with. She's called me every name in the book, which is sort of ironic given that she is such a devout Catholic, but I'm sure she asked for forgiveness and the big man gave it to her, so all is well. She often turns to "I have to tell you how I feel." Uh, no, you don't. You really can keep some thoughts and feelings to yourself. Thankfully, there's some balance to her. Just when you can't take her criticism any more, she'll do something amazing like one of her widely celebrated farts.

Seriously. We, her family, have been in awe of her wind valve for decades. Early in the morning, late at night, and everywhere in between, this little lady can rip ass. It's astonishing. Most people think it's an embellishment and I understand why, but miraculously I captured one of my mom's massive gas releases on video and shared it with the world. She's understandably not thrilled about it, but I consider it payback for her way of interacting with the rest of us. It's all over the internet and has been featured on dozens of channels because it truly is an other-level fart. A friend said he timed it at 9.12 seconds. I told him she's had better ones. It's true. I have an after-market exhaust on my car that I paid a fortune for, and it doesn't come close to notes she can reach with her horn.

I can already hear how she'll react to this chapter.

"The things you write about your own mother. Que Dios te perdone." (May God forgive you.)

"You know I love you, Mom."

"Yah, sure, Tommy."

"Come on, Mom."

"You're going to have to *pay* for this one."

"Oh yeah, what are we talking here?"

"You put it in a book, Tommy. I still can't find a car."

America's Most Wanted

I moved to Washington, DC, on September 10, 2001, to begin my first "showbiz" job. You now know that during college I had interned at *America's Most Wanted*, the long-running show that profiled and led to the capture of some of the most dangerous people on earth. Soon after graduating, they offered me a job and I accepted.

The first day they set me up in an office that was already occupied by another guy named Tom. So the two Toms were kept together in one place. It was a lot of Tom. The other Tom knew it and referred to our space as "T squared" and "T2." The other Tom was an on-air reporter. He would go into the field and be seen on TV talking about one of these horrific human beings we were profiling. My job was a lot shittier.

I had the fun task of being a researcher. I had to find fugitives for us to chase. Basically, I would look up who had jumped bail or who had eluded authorities and then I would get as much info on the person as possible before pitching to our story editor why we should do a segment on said fugitive. It might sound kind of cool, but what you can't gather is just how somber and depressing it is to research felons for twelve hours a day.

One particularly epic piece of shit had been convicted of child sex crimes in Honduras and Costa Rica, but as is customary down there, he was able to bribe his way out. He was American and we wanted to send his ass back to prison in Costa Rica. That was enough info for us to pursue him, but in this asshole's case there was also a diary. This scum of the earth detailed his stalking, seducing, and sexual exploits with children. If you ever want to feel nauseated, read a child predator's diary.

I pitched that we should go after this guy, and we did. They sent me to Costa Rica to work as a translator for the episode, and to this day I don't know if we got him because I left the show after that week. I had already left DC and had just started settling down in Los Angeles to pursue my showbiz dreams. While I was down in Costa Rica I had to interview several different people for the show. I had a producer, cameraman, audio guy, and a local guide with me. Our first interview was an American man who dedicated his life to saving and helping young women who had been abused. He was so committed to this cause that he moved there and never left. Costa Rica has legal prostitution, but economic inequities have led to a lot of exploitation of underage girls. This man's life was saving these young, abused girls. Next, they had me interview a victim who had been kidnapped, assaulted, impregnated, and neglected. Her story was so extreme and stunning that as she told me what happened to her, I cried. At first it was just a little bit. My eyes welled up and I was trying to make it go away. This girl was completely composed while she talked about the brutal things she suffered; the least I could do was hold it together. I looked up, I looked down, and then I looked at her, and the tears rolled down my cheeks, one or two to start and then the stream flowed. There was a brief moment where I thought she was going to stop telling her story but she didn't, thankfully. She kept going and she let me cry about it. Afterward my cameraman put his hand on my shoulder and gave me a little squeeze, partially to comfort me, but also it had a bit of "this might not be for you."

AMW wasn't all bad, though. I got to spend a good deal of time at the White House, which is a thrill at that age. After 9/11 we started sending reporters to the lawn outside the West Wing. If that doesn't make sense to you, think about it. After 9/11 who became the *Most Wanted* person in the world? Bin Laden. And why the White House? Well, they couldn't stop talking about it either. On television you see White House reporters posted up in the same area on the lawn. Every network and news channel has someone standing there. I would call people and tell them where I was.

"I'm at the White House. No, literally. I'm standing fifty yards from the West Wing on the lawn."

I would go on about how close I was to the president and his family. I'd make jokes about snipers and national security. I didn't realize that we were being listened to outside on the lawn until a producer told me. I could not have been the only dumb young guy saying stupid shit on the White House grounds, but I sure felt like the loudest one in that moment.

A lot of it was cool, but also something was pretty clear to me. I didn't want to do this job for the rest of my life. I love crime stories. I love reading about them and I love watching the shows about them, but I didn't love meeting the victims. It was all too much. I can still see that girl in Costa Rica. Even with all the jokes that I make about crimes and chaos on my podcast, they can't cover how soft I am. They can't mask that I'll break down crying if the person in front of me shares a tragic story about their life. I've made jokes about murder and plotting to kidnap someone. I've gone into detail about how to evade capture and what to consider when planning a homicide, but it's not something I want to do. It's a fantasy world.

That's the one thing that I feel like so many comedy fans get wrong. There's this widespread belief that any joke a comedian makes is rooted in truth, that if a comedian says anything, on a deeper level the comic must feel that way. This could not be more inaccurate. What is true is that a comedian will say *anything* if they think it's funny, and sometimes, *sometimes* there's truth in the joke. A lot of times there isn't. I remember early on inviting a girl to see me do stand-up. While onstage, I had a joke about peeing on someone. I don't remember exactly what I said or how I got there, but I do remember saying, "And then I peed on 'em." It was a joke. Not a brilliant joke, but nevertheless a joke. It was absurd to say in the context of what I was describing. Also, it was completely made up. I didn't actually pee on anyone. It was also an effective statement to say onstage. I know this because everybody laughed and I kept it in my act during that time. See, that's the thing we care about most—did people laugh? If they did, then I'll *keep saying that.* After the show the girl and I hung out, and she could not stop saying, "Now I know you like to pee on people... That's your thing, huh?" etc.

At first I laughed, but then it became apparent that she really believed it, and she couldn't stop referencing it with a knowing look in her eye, like she'd cracked the case of the Piss Stalker. I broke it down that it wasn't true, and then she thought I was ashamed, like I was now denying my deep, dark secret that was masked in jokes. She wanted me to know that it was okay and that she was okay with my kink. She kept telling me it was okay that I was into pee. I kept saying that I wasn't, but it didn't matter. She was convinced that she had uncovered this secret through her elite psychological instincts, something I've encountered *countless* times during conversations with casual stand-up fans. I was so annoyed with this chick that I'm embarrassed to say I did something I'd never done before—I peed on her. And much to my surprise, I really did enjoy it. If we ever meet and you want to give me a treat, don't offer to buy me a drink. Let me pee on you.

Serena Williams

I was trying to stuff my bag in the overhead compartment. They designed those things to minimize the amount of stuff you can bring on board with you. Why? They want you to check that bag, because if you check that bag, you pay and they win. I ain't havin' that shit. I. Stuff. That. Bag. Every time.

Just as I was getting the bag with all my shit into the compartment that didn't want it I heard, "Excuse me," very politely said.

I turned, saw the woman standing outside the row I was in, and I immediately said, "You're the greatest."

I said that because I was looking at Serena Williams aka the greatest. I don't think I'd ever been as starstruck.

As we took off I couldn't help myself. I made small talk. "I can't believe I'm sitting next to you."

"Well, you are." She was fun and clearly not taking herself too seriously. I asked if she lived in LA, and she told me she was only visiting because Florida was her primary home. Once we were at cruising altitude she opened her laptop and began taking notes. Lots of notes in a pad. After a while I asked what she was doing.

"School."

"School? You're in school?"

"Yeahhh. I'm taking classes."

It never occurred to me that a superstar athlete might want to further their education, but at that moment I thought, *Oh yeah, you can keep learning even when you're successful. Cool.*

We ended up talking a good while before she asked what I did. This is, of course, the norm on flights. People *always* ask what you do, and it doesn't take long for comedians to realize that it's not a good idea to tell strangers you're a comedian. If you don't know why, imagine how *you* would react if the person sitting next to you said that they were *a comedian.* You're probably not done asking questions, right? When you're first starting out it's kind of cool to tell people. I mean you're new to it too. It's affirmation that you're actually doing it, for real. It doesn't take long for you to put together that if you tell people you work in comedy, they're going to talk to you for the rest of the flight. And they're going to have a lot to say. I've heard every type of question and comment from all types.

Comedy? I love comedy! You know, people say I'm pretty funny. What kind of comedy do you do? Tell me a joke. Do you curse?

Are you on Saturday Night Live? *I love* SNL. *Kristen Wiig was my favorite. Do you watch it?*

Who are your favorite comics? What's your style like? Have you seen this thing in the news with Syria? How would you joke about that?

Oops, I spilled on myself. I guess that's going in your act, huh?

Yeah, I can't wait to get to the stage tonight to tell them how you spilled coffee on your pants.

Most working comedians develop a reflex for dismissing any notion they're a comedian on flights. I either say I work in "production" and like "creating schedules" or I say I work as a consultant in construction. Most people don't have a lot of follow-ups on that. One time I thought I was clever and said I worked with "pens" as in the manufacturing of pens, and the guy had so many goddamn questions about pens, so I dropped that one.

But when Serena Williams asks what you do, you tell her the truth. Not just because it's the right thing to do, but in this case, her asking me questions was welcomed. I was cool, but not *too* cool with it.

"I'm a comedian."

Her reply?

"Anywhere I can watch you?"

I mean, that is the *perfect* response.

And I had the perfect reply. It was about a year after my first one-hour special had come out.

"I have a special on Netflix called *Completely Normal*." She smiled and, get this, she wrote it down on her notepad. Then I spelled my name out and watched her write that down too.

It was a pretty cool moment. When we landed I asked her for a pic, which she was very sweet about. "I mean I don't have on makeup and we just flew, but...okay."

I was extremely pleased with myself as I walked through the airport toward ground transportation. I imagined Serena Williams would be watching my special *Completely Normal* that night.

Fuck!

At *that* moment it hit me. In that special I actually *talk about* Serena Williams! And what I say is *exactly* this:

"Oh, my God. I do think about death. I just want it to be

justified, you know? Like, if I die violently, you know, maybe I have, like, Serena Williams sitting on my face, and...I don't know, Venus is polishing me off, and they're trying to fit a racket in my ass or something like that. Then my wife comes in, boom, and I'm, like, fucking done."

Keep in mind I wasn't saying this in an interview. It was *during a stand-up performance.* During stand-up we exaggerate, often in extreme ways, which is why a lot of people laugh. It's not what you ever say in regular conversation. That's the magic of a stand-up performance. In the act I was talking about only wanting to die if it were justified, worth it. Still, I was appalled, not that I'd said it, but that it could be interpreted by her as a not so *hidden* message from me.

"Hey, watch my special. I think you'll like it." Wink-wink!

It was absolutely not my intention to do that. I think both of the Williams sisters are lovely, inspiring, super-talented athletes, and what I say on the stage is not meant to translate into the real world. I really had forgotten about that bit, and now I had to process that I'd suggested to this woman I admire that she watch me talk about a threesome with her and her sister and an enormous apparatus shoved up my ass right before I die.

At that moment I *wanted* to die.

Of course, I never heard from Serena, but earlier this year I did run into her. I realize how casual I made that sound.

Ran into Serena at the store. Nice gal!

Not what I mean. I *cannot believe* that I ran into her after a show. She and her husband, who, I'm sure, didn't tell her he wanted to die the same way I did, were a few feet ahead of me at a party. I was drunk *and* high when I spotted them—the perfect combination when you want to relive an embarrassing story with someone. I approached the two of them fifteen feet from the bar and held them captive as I retold the entire story above. My intention was to make them laugh. And it worked with Alexis, her husband, who was ear-to-ear smiling. Serena was politely listening, not as entertained as I'd hoped. Was it because she *did watch* and was remembering the bit? I felt a sweat start to build. It's one that I've felt before.

Am I bombing?

At one point I could feel the shame working its way from my face down my body and I said to them, in a not-so-quiet voice, "I think I'm humiliating myself right now . . . I've been drinking."

To which Serena replied, "We're trying to get on your level. Where can we get a drink?"

I pointed to the bar.

I'm making you a promise. If I *ever* run into Serena Williams again I am *not* bringing any of this up.

Road Dog

There's no business like show business. And if show business doesn't want you, there's always comedy. Nothing can truly prepare you for life as a road comic. People see successful comics and naturally assume that it's awesome. It is. It's great to have people want to come out to see you do what you chose to do in life. It's great to get paid well and fly comfortably and stay in nice hotels. But it takes most of us who do this a long, *long* time to get there. Hundreds and thousands of shows. I mean it. So many countless, awful hours doing so many awful shows. On the way up you suffer in more ways than one, and I wouldn't change anything about my experience. Here I present to you my top five list of the most glamorous things about being a stand-up comedian.

5. You'll share a shitty condo with someone you don't know, and they might not be the best roommate.

Comedy clubs are famously cheap. They sling wings and beers, and they're not known for paying well. Before you get to the level where you stay in hotels, you stay in what is known as a "comedy condo." It's essentially an apartment or condo that the club has purchased. They normally are quite negligent of the property. They don't really clean it well or maintain it in a way that would make you want to reside there. It *is*, however, a tax write-off for the scumbag owner of the club who also happens to own that condo. By making the comedians stay there he is writing off the cost of the property as a business expense. These places are impressively shitty. They are dated, with furniture that was clearly bought whenever the property was purchased: ten, fifteen, twenty years before. Carpets with cigarette burns, televisions with no remote, and the worst of all—bedroom windows with no curtains or blinds. This is a particularly egregious crime, as most comedians don't go to bed until well after midnight when working a club, and without curtains, well, you can imagine. No one wants a well-lit bedroom when they're trying to sleep the morning away. All the condos I stayed at were garbage with the exception of Wende Curtis's condo in downtown Denver. She owns the Comedy Works clubs and a host of other businesses, and since she actually values the comedians she puts on her stages, she spent over $1 million purchasing and renovating a condo for the performers to stay in. Again, she is the rare exception.

I once shared a condo with a 600-pound man. That is *not* an exaggeration. It was an astonishing experience to be that close to someone in that body. Normally you only see it when the good people at the TLC network launch a new show: *1000-Lb. Sisters*, *My 600 Pound Life*, or my favorite of theirs, *Fat Black Midgets*. This guy was a very troubled, but extremely funny comic. He was a single dad working the road like the rest of us. I shared the condo with him that weekend and I'll never forget it. He was absolutely enormous. The craziest part—the condo had one bathroom. We both bathed and relieved ourselves in the same space. When he shit, the smell would penetrate the walls. If you think I'm suggesting that a super obese person's bowels smell worse than the average person's, you are correct. I've never been around anything like it. In the mornings when I wanted to go out for breakfast, I would knock on his door and ask if he wanted to come with me. He said he did and that he just needed a "minute." It would take him forty-five minutes just to get out of the room. It was sad, of course. One time, we walked into a restaurant and before I sat down, I turned and noticed he was gone. I went outside and he was already getting into the car.

"What are you doing?"

"They only have booths in there. Can't fit," and we'd be off to look for a restaurant with tables and chairs.

Damn.

I'd never thought of that. I thought of *myself* as fat, but I never had to leave a place because I couldn't fit. He was clearly used to it, but I was taken aback.

As eye-opening as that weekend was, the one that left me a little terrified was when I was paired up with an older opening act. He was resentful that I was headlining as that had been his job a few years back. It's something that happens in the world of comedy and entertainment. You rise, plateau, and then decline. I'm hyperaware that it can happen to me, and I'm always extremely polite to upperclassmen in my field. With this guy it became obvious almost immediately that he was a big-time drinker. Some comics will have a drink before going onstage and a whole lot like to drink after the show, but this was different. This guy started at noon and he only drank whiskey. We went to have lunch, as is typical for comics working a weekend together, and he abruptly shifted the conversation from comedy to whether or not I liked my wife.

"I do."

"Is she smart?"

"She is."

"Well, mine's about as dumb as they make 'em."

I laughed it off as an older guy venting about his longtime marriage. Then that Saturday after the late show we went back to the condo. He was fifteen drinks deep. We were watching COPS and it must have been at least two a.m.

"You ever see the Paris Hilton sex tape?" seemed like an odd segue, but I had no reason to lie to him.

"Uh, yeah. I think we all did."

"That guy's got a nice cock on him."

"Never really thought about it."

"I mean I'm sure he didn't mind that getting out there."

"Right."

"I mean there's a lot of chicks to bang out there, but there's a lot of guys too."

What the *fuck*. I froze as my new reality hit me. This guy wants to fuck *me* and he's hammered. I felt like reacting would be a bad move, so I sat still and just stared at the TV. I told myself that any sudden movement would escalate the situation, so I decided at the commercial break I would go to my room. A few minutes passed and, thankfully, a commercial came on and I did just that. Nothing was said. Once I was inside the room my fear kicked in again. This guy weighed 100 pounds less than me, but I still was in a state of panic. I pushed the dresser in front of my bedroom door, then the nightstand, then a chair. I needed fair warning if this maniac tried to come in. Was this drunk creeper going to try something? Not a chance I'd be falling asleep anytime soon. I lay in bed wide-eyed. Hours later I passed out.

The next morning, I got up and he was gone.

4. You might not get paid.

This might shock you when you read the *Forbes* list of the top-earning comics in the world, but if that list went on it would show a severe drop. Most comedians barely make a living. Barely. A large number of them have part-time jobs while they try to make it as a comic. I was one of those guys for a while. I worked in restaurants, on set for TV/film productions doing various menial jobs, and at a spa. If you're not clear why a working comedian who just performed in front of a packed house needs *another* job, let me break it down for you. *Most* comedy clubs across the United States operate the same way. There's an MC who opens the show, greets the audience, and returns to the stage to introduce each comic and make club announcements. This comedian is usually paid fifty dollars per show. That's the same rate they were paid in 1990. The feature or "middle" act usually does twenty minutes of stand-up. This comedian is usually paid a hundred per show. And then the headliner, the person whose name is on the marquee and presumably who all the people are there to see, well, that has a sliding scale. On the low end it might be $1,000 for six shows. Keep in mind you don't work every weekend, so if you headline two weekends at that rate you're essentially making $500 a week, and you *need* another job.

One comedy club manager gave me shit for not going long enough in the middle spot. I did twenty-two instead of twenty-five minutes. She insulted me all weekend long. "I thought you were supposed to be funny." And after all her bullshit, I get back to LA and the check bounces. Nothing makes you feel quite as empty as not getting paid after a bad week. I worked at a pizza place in the San Fernando Valley to make ends meet. I dug a ditch once. I'm not saying I was a ditch digger, but I did dig the one. It was for a super-rich guy in Bel-Air. A friend had referred me over for some construction work since I had done some one summer during college. When I got to this massive house, I thought I'd be laying tile or passing cinder blocks up a line. Nope.

"Dig a ditch there."

"Where?"

"Right there." I looked up and saw the order wasn't coming from a contractor. This was the owner. Had to be. He was wearing slacks, a button-down shirt with the top two buttons open, *and* he was holding a little white Maltese. We had one when I was a kid. I complimented his dog and then asked for some clarity.

"Sir, you want a ditch right here next to the house."

"I've got some big plans for it."

For the ditch? Okay.

He left, and the contractor showed up about fifteen minutes later. All the other guys were doing labor *in* the house, but I had a shovel and was doing what I was told.

"The fuck are you doing?"

"Digging a ditch."

"Mind telling me why?"

"The owner told me he wanted it here, so I just started digging."

"He?"

"Yup. Came right up to me with his dog and said to dig right here."

"The owner of this house is a woman. Fill that fuckin' hole up."
Okay!

3. Oh, the places you'll go.

I've had countless conversations with strangers about the fact that I'm a stand-up comic. Almost every one of those conversations leads to the stranger saying something to the effect of, "It must be so great to travel and see the world!" I can tell their own fantasies of globetrotting are playing in their heads, not realizing that we are business travelers, going anywhere and everywhere. Winnipeg in the winter, Phoenix in the summer. I've performed at music festivals, dive bars, parking lots, and minor league baseball games. I've done long weeks in some real shitholes, and I've *even* gone as far as doing stand-up comedy in Guantanamo Bay. Yup, Gitmo.

You probably heard about it on the news. After 9/11 the United States began scooping up and shipping out a lot of bad guys and some guys they weren't so sure about to this naval base in Cuba. Within the base there's a prison. That's all I knew about it: that terrorists like Khalid Sheik Mohammed were there and that it *has* to be awful. So when I got the call saying, "Do you want to do some shows in Guantanamo?" I thought, *Are they really trying to entertain a prison camp?*

Then they told me something that for some reason I couldn't picture: Gitmo is a base, and the prison is a very small part of it. So, we're not entertaining the prisoners? No.

I flew to Fort Lauderdale and then jumped on a US Navy plane with a few other comics, and we landed at the base with some serious anxiety. What the hell did we just agree to do?

We were greeted by uniformed personnel and told that our

group would have to split up. Two of us would go to the regular housing and two of us would have to go "elsewhere." I was put in the "elsewhere" group, which turned out to be housing for Naval officers, CIA, and other US intelligence officers who were temporarily on-site. It was, as I later found out, much more desirable housing. It had wifi and decent bedding and... CIA officers! I felt like I was on an official, top-secret mission. After a short period of settling in, I was told to meet a guide in the lobby of the building. I took the elevator and shared it with a man about twenty years older than me. He had a slight build, a serious look on his face, and a mustache. He was wearing shorts, a t-shirt, and sneakers and was clearly going out for exercise. I tried to talk him up. "How's it going?"

His eyes barely looked at me.

"I'm here doing shows." The elevator hit the lobby and he exited. I can't ever remember being dissed so quietly and efficiently in my life. And I wasn't the least bit insulted. I thought, *That's how CIA guys must be. Awesome.*

Once in the van with our guide, we were given a tour of the base. We had all braced ourselves for some seriously depressing, "You ain't in Kansas anymore" shit, but what we discovered was... KFC. They had the colonel's chicken, a Subway, post office, parks, a high school, and, oh yeah, kids. A bunch of kids whose parents live and work on base. The shows ended up being incredible. Everyone was so appreciative and enthusiastic. It really made me feel like we were doing something of substance just by going there and entertaining these dedicated sailors, soldiers, and marines. A few days later we flew out and went back to our homes. A month later I was in Atlanta playing a club, and in the lobby of my hotel I saw a face that I recognized.

Now, I travel a lot, so I do see and meet a ton of people, but this face was bugging me. It was like I was certain I had seen this man, but I couldn't quite place where I knew him from. I was staring, wondering, and then it hit me: Gitmo. This was the guy who I rode the elevator with. The one who didn't even acknowledge me when I tried speaking to him. So what did I do? I walked over to him.

"Hey, I recognize you."

He just stared at me, stone-faced.

"I was at Gitmo last month in the officers' building. We rode the elevator together."

Before I had finished my sentence, he had turned his back to me and walked away. Now I really felt fear for the first time. What the fuck is wrong with me? Of all the people I could tap on the shoulder and say "hey" to, I pick a guy who *maybe* sets up black op sites and possibly teaches people how to waterboard.

That was my first and last trip to Gitmo and the last time I ever acknowledged a stranger.

2. Some people will hate you (and that's a good thing).

When you start doing stand-up the only feedback you get is usually positive. I mean, you're terrible, but people can tell that you're not experienced, so they take it easy on you. It's friends and supportive types who go to these "bringer" shows (shows where you, the performer, are supposed to literally "bring" people to watch it). They tend to be like parents at a kindergarten talent show: "Hey, way to go! I can't believe you even have the balls to get up there." As you progress into more professional shows with real audiences, you certainly have a sense about when you did well and when you didn't. Some comics remain delusional, but even they know the truth. No matter what happens at live shows, nothing can quite prepare you for what the digital age has brought into our everyday life—the comments. When your comedy is posted online, you want everyone to see it. When people start seeing it, they start leaving comments, and *ohhhh, boy*, you are *not* ready.

"You suck."

"Don't quit your day job."

"I've been to funerals that were funnier."

Your heart drops, you sink. Why are people being mean to me? By now you know that the internet is a vast wasteland, and if you're looking for care and comfort you might want to reconsider looking for it online. As your profile grows as a comedian, you will gain more fans and people who aren't into you, and some of those people feel the need to tell you.

Posting a video on YouTube is one thing, but having a worldwide release on Netflix is another. You are literally at 140 million subscribers' mercy. And when you lean aggressively into a joke or just joke about something, *anything* that someone takes personally, you will be hearing from some of them. Seems easy to say, "Well, just ignore them." It's true and it's good advice, but it's much easier said than done. Comedians are comedians for a reason. We didn't get the approval we were seeking as children. We want validation—every day. Every show is not just a show and a place for us to try jokes. It's a place to get the affirmation we're on an endless journey to obtain. When you first read the hate, don't let anyone fool you, it sucks and it hurts. You eventually get used to it. One of my friends likes to say, "It's snake venom. You take a little bit and build up a tolerance to it, and then one day it doesn't affect you."

It took me years and years to get there, and now I can say with full confidence that I accept it as part of the job. You're never going to win everyone over. Not everyone is going to think you're funny or like you. And just like not every movie is for everyone, neither is every comic. I do think it makes sense for people not to agree on who is funny or what is funny. It's completely subjective, and we all have different experiences to inform our opinions. Hate mail also means that more people are learning who you are; you're becoming more famous. Really famous people get tons of hate thrown their way. Think about it. Taylor Swift, Brad Pitt, and Scarlett Johansson are wildly famous and without question receive tons of adulation and also more hate mail than you or I. That being said, you're still a complete asshole and total psycho if you go to any artist's social media or website and send them messages about how you don't like their song or movie or joke. I'm trying to imagine doing that. I can't even imagine being friends with someone who would openly admit that they do that.

After years and years of growing accustomed to it, I learned to at least have a little fun with it. When my Netflix special *Disgraceful* debuted, I was bombarded with hate mail on every platform: Twitter, Facebook, Instagram, and my website. Every hour I could go to any of those and there would be a hundred new messages in each, thousands per day! Day after day the number was growing. A huge portion of them were coming from Louisiana. I had joked in the special that I met a man from Lafayette, which I did. We had a difficult-to-understand conversation because his accent was ridiculous. The bit then shifts to me railing against Cajun people and stating that I don't understand why they have rights. Then I state that we should build a wall in this country, but we should build it around their state. You get it. It was harsh, but you know, comedy.

So many people were enraged and contacting me about my Louisiana jokes that I decided the best thing to do was keep them writing, so I pretended to be Blake, Tom Segura's "assistant" in charge of running his social media. I mean *my* social media. The following is a real exchange via the Messenger app on Facebook. A lady messaged me:

Just had to let you know that not everyone from Louisiana is moronic. We do not all speak as though we are holding marbles in our mouths! You are a douchebag for that "joke." People in Louisiana liked you. Fuck you, sir! Go chew an aspirin.

And "Blake" replied:

Heather! My goodness. I'm Blake. I work for Tom and monitor his social media. What's this aspirin thing about?

She replied:

Aspirin tastes bad...like Tom's dumb jokes. Let him read the message. Hell, read it to his ancient ass. Sorry to hear you have to monitor his social media. I work for an asshole also.

Blake:

You have no idea. Tom is the worst. One time I brought him an iced coffee with too little ice. Turns out he likes extra ice. You know what he did? He made me stay awake for 3 days! Ugh. I was so angry. It made me sick. I had to see a psychiatrist. He said it was punishment for bringing the wrong kind of caffeine and since I wasn't helping him stay awake he was going to force me to stay awake. He made me stay at his house and he'd play loud music and turn all these lights on. And then he had his friend Capital J basically torture me. He's such a jerk!

Lady:

OMG! I'm so sorry, you seem cool. And I love your name.

Blake:

Thanks! I like your name too. I want to quit this job but it's hard with bills and all. I just have to read all this stuff and reply and only pass on certain ones to him. Sometimes if I pass on the wrong message, I get punished for that too. One time he poured hot wax from a candle in my ears. He thought ear wax, candle wax—what's the difference? But the candle wax was so hot it damaged my ear canal and ear drum. At least he bought me some nice hearing aids tho. But I have permanent hearing loss thanks to him.

Lady:

Man, he's more of an asshole than I thought! So sorry. You should send me a friend request. We can be friends if you like.

Blake:

Oh yeah he's a much bigger asshole off stage. Thanks for letting me vent. I'll never forgive him for what he did to my brother. He promised to make him s'mores on Halloween and my brother who is 7 was so excited but Tom thought it'd be hilarious to make them with hallucinogens. Now my brother only speaks using numbers. It's out of this world. Instead of saying "I'm hungry" he'll say "268 493 1171." It took forever for us to understand what the hell it means. He goes to a therapist 5 days a week to learn words again. Tom pays for it but still, my parents are so upset.

Lady:

That's evil! wow, I'm so sorry! Your poor baby bro! That's heartbreaking. Well, I have no problem at all with you venting! I vented to you didn't I? How old are you?

Blake:

I'm 27. He's terrifying. Thanks for listening.

Lady:

OK. Don't let him walk over you.

Blake:

Yeah I'll try. He made me wear this protective suit so he could try out some martial arts stuff he's learning, but I'm much smaller than him. He separated my right shoulder. Since I had to wear a sling he told me to pretend to be a 3-legged dog. Had to eat out of a bowl and sit in a cage like a dog. He's nuts! But he pays well.

Lady:

Oh my God! Wow, Blake... You're a stronger person than me! I thought my boss was an asshole! Now I feel blessed. Look, if you ever want someone to talk to, I'm here. You seem like a cool person. You don't deserve that crap!

Blake:

Thanks! He keeps stockpiling guns and playing with bullets in front of the staff here. Makes me anxious. He shot at a Fed Ex guy and somehow got out of it. Pretty crazy. And the cops love him. They let him put police lights and a siren on his car cause he donated so much.

Lady:

What a shithead! That's not cool! I'm kinda glad his joke pissed me off now. He's so uncool anyway. You seem to be though. I wonder how you put up with it!

Blake:

I just need the job. It's a job and sometimes he can be cool—pays for dinner and stuff but then he'll make me give him pedicures and I have to wash his underwear by hand. One time he locked me in an outhouse at his uncle's place in Idaho. The smell was unbearable. Plus, I'm diabetic so I had some real trouble stabilizing without food for that long. That was another hospital stay because of him. But he got me this cool Harry Potter collection which I love so I forgave him.

End of convo.

1. You might die.

The road can kill you. You're not in your home city and you have everything at your disposal: food, booze, drugs, sex, and crowds that want to give you all those things. You can go down a dark path if you choose to. It sounds dramatic, but it's true. I know people who have eaten, drank, and drugged themselves to death. While a lot of people see "doing comedy" as fun, the road can be a very lonely place. You need to work at not falling apart, and the older you get, the harder you have to work at it. In 2006 I quit my last full-time job working as a post-production coordinator on reality TV shows. That job entails a lot of organizing and scheduling the "post" needs for the shows. I quit the day I signed with my manager. I shouldn't have quit so abruptly, but I was excited and told myself that I was now doing this *for real*. I would now be full-time as a comedian. No longer would this be something I dabbled in at night or on the weekends with the security of a real, full-time job to back me up.

I went on the road almost every week. I took everything that was offered to me. Most of it was "feature" work, $100 a show (still the *same* rate today), usually six shows a week with no airfare included. That means a lot of times I was netting *maybe* $200 a week, maybe less. I had to accrue debt. As the year went on, I told myself that there was no turning back. I would not stop trying to make it as a comic now, but the reality of my situation was stressful. You can't force more work or a raise at this point in your career. You just have to go along with it and build your proficiency as it comes. It's probably the hardest part of the whole journey: accepting that you're doing all you can and that it's barely enough.

By the end of 2006, I had gained thirty pounds. The next year I put on twenty more. The weight maintenance battle is one that I've always fought and I was losing it, badly. I was eating like shit, going to bed at 3:00 a.m. and getting up at noon and never, ever exercising.

In 2009, I played a pickup game of basketball. I used to play pickup games at the YMCA in Hollywood all the time when I first arrived. Some ballers and really scrappy dudes would play. We would play for hours. This 2009 game was seven years later. It was unexpected and a real wake-up call. If you know me, you're probably thinking of another basketball event and wondering if this encounter tops "that one." No, we will get to the special one later.

In 2009, I was hanging with comics on the road, and there happened to be a court next to our hotel. I had really devolved into a slow, fat, sloppy bag of dog shit.

That 2009 game started as a shoot-around. Everyone was just loosely having fun, but the familiar feeling of playing ball woke up the athletic dude buried deep beneath my many layers of fat. Instead of playing HORSE I insisted that we play 21. Three of us would battle for every shot, every point. There was the typical running, jumping, pivoting, and shoving that goes on in any basketball game, but it was all happening to a body that hadn't moved in half a decade. A body that was decidedly slower, weaker, and totally unprepared to take on this task.

I played terribly that day. I was glad we did it because it felt good to sweat, play a game, and just compete. What I was not prepared for was what my body would do in response. The next morning, I woke up in pain. Real pain. There's "I banged my knee" on the cabinet and then there's "Something is wrong. I can't move" pain. This was the latter. The pain in my back was so severe that I had tears in my eyes. I couldn't sit up. I couldn't walk, sit, or stand. It was all encompassing. I held on to the wall, telling the other guys that I didn't think I could perform that night. They asked if I wanted to go to the hospital. I considered it, but decided that I needed to rest. One of the guys tried to crack my back—it didn't help. They kept trying to figure out *what* exactly was hurt. Was it nerve damage, skeletal?

I had gotten so out of shape that merely playing a casual game of basketball made my back hurt like I had fought someone in the ring. It took me days to get back to normal, and I knew that I had let myself go. It woke me up to get back to working out and eating better, and 2010 was somewhat of a turnaround for me. I lost some weight and then shot my Comedy Central half-hour special.

It wouldn't be the end of reminding myself to stay healthy, though. That's a constant. It took the birth of my first son to remind me, "Don't get reckless and die." This time I lost fifty pounds and have kept *most* of it off. I have two kids now, and so the reminder is daily. That and the comics who are no longer with us: Greg Giraldo, Ralphie May, Mitch Hedberg, Chris Farley, Patrice O'Neal, Brody Stevens, and so many more. I hear a voice sometimes telling me, "Take care of yourself. Don't be reckless and die."

Bank Shot

I moved to Los Angeles when I was twenty-two years old. I just wanted to perform comedy in some way. I thought acting was the natural path for me. I'd done improv and sketch when I was in high school, though only for one summer. I had a small part in a community play, also during my high school years, and I'd shot countless comedy videos with my friends. I knew I could do it. I was funny, I could access emotions, and I was also really good at memorizing. So here was my plan. I'd read that a number of *Saturday Night Live* stars had been trained at the Groundlings, an improv school in Los Angeles. In my mind all I needed to do was train there, get on *SNL,* and then after a few seasons I'd do movies.

Solid plan, Tom.

LA is a huge city full of people looking to find their way among the millions of others who *seem* to know what they're doing. There, I felt like I had no one, because I didn't. I needed a friend. At the Groundlings school I became *friendly* with some of the other students. Still, I wouldn't become close with any of them. They already had their own crew.

I wasn't a friendless loser forever, though. The Groundlings led me to stand-up, and it was stand-up that would lead me to some of the closest relationships I've ever had. The first great friend I made in Los Angeles was Ryan Sickler. Ryan hails from Baltimore, one of the country's toughest cities, and he has that city in his DNA. He'll talk shit as hard as anyone I've ever met, but at his core he is a sweet, caring guy. Ryan is a few years older than me and already had his bearings in LA when we met. He introduced me to comedy show bookers, took me to all his favorite food spots, and invited me to hang out at his place. I more than accepted the welcome. I practically moved in. I don't think he was anticipating having me there, at his place, every day, but that's just the kind of guy I am. If I like you, I will come around.

Ryan had a great setup: a nice apartment, but more importantly, he always had the latest PlayStation, and we would sometimes play until sunrise. We played like Sony was paying us to test their games. God, I miss having no responsibilities! *Madden*, *Halo*, and *Splinter Cell* were on regular rotation.

I started dating my wife, Christina, in 2005, but Ryan has had a series of girlfriends, some for one night, others for a few years. Whenever he was single I'd keep my eyes open for him. Over time I learned his type: pretty, curvy, funny, with a preference for Latinas and Black women.

So it came as no surprise when, a few years ago, I was standing in line at a Wells Fargo branch and thought of Ryan immediately when I saw that the woman behind the counter was a beautiful, olive-skinned woman.

Damn, Ryan would dig her.

When I approached the counter I became even more convinced. She had a big, beautiful smile, and best of all, she was fun.

"Just making a deposit."

"You leaving any for me?"

"You know, if I had more I would."

When I left I called him right away.

"Hey, man, I think I found your next girlfriend."

"Who?"

"She's a teller at Wells Fargo. Absolutely gorgeous. Olive-skinned, curvy, and a great attitude."

"Shit, I like that."

"Want me to try to set it up?"

"You got a picture?"

Of the bank teller? Yeah, right next to the pictures of my butcher and the mailman.

"No, but she's smoking hot. Trust me."

"Kinda need to see her first."

"Seriously, you don't trust me?"

"I don't do blind dates."

Can you believe this shit? Here I am thinking of my single friend, *knowing* that I'm looking at a woman he'd like, and he hits me with "I *need* to see a picture first."

Fine.

I let it go. A few weeks later I was back at the same branch in the same line, looking at tweets on my phone, when I saw her again. She looked even better. Without thinking, I hit the camera app, raised my phone and snapped a few pictures of her.

Now he'll see.

Once again, I was impressed with her conversational skills. I mean, she noticed my shoes.

"Are those Jordans?"

"You know it."

"I've never seen those colors before."

"That's because a friend of mine made them."

"I need a friend like that."

When a lady compliments your J's, she's a keeper. This time I noticed her name tag, *Natasha*. I was absolutely certain that he would like her, but I didn't say anything to her. I wanted Ryan's blessing on her photo first.

I left the bank and realized that I was running late. The branch was located adjacent to downtown in the southeast pocket of Koreatown, and I had to get to the Icehouse, a comedy club in Pasadena, which with traffic, could end up taking me sixty to seventy minutes at this early evening hour. No more than five minutes passed when I got a call from a number I didn't recognize. I usually don't answer those, but this day I did.

"Hello."

"Tom Segura?"

"Yes."

"This is Carlos with Wells Fargo."

I was impressed. You usually don't get customer service follow-ups this quickly, but I was happy to tell them how well they were doing.

"Hi, Carlos. I'm very happy with my accounts and with the service I've received."

"I'm from the security division of Wells Fargo. Is there a reason you were taking photos inside the branch today? We have you on video."

Everything slowed down. I felt my voice drop, and my vision blurred.

Am I having an aneurysm?

My first instinct was to try to defuse the situation with a light-hearted question.

"Oh, I mean, did you think I took them to rob the bank?"

"I don't know, did you?"

What kind of fucking idiot am I, volunteering that? Do you think I'm going to rob *you?*

"No. No, I wasn't and I'm not planning on...ever robbing your or any other bank."

"So why were you taking pictures?"

"I was taking a photo of the teller so I could show her to my friend...for a potential date."

Fuck. That can't sound good.

"So you were taking photos of the teller?"

"Yeah, I think her name is Natasha. Sorry."

"Sir, we don't appreciate our employees' privacy being violated."

"Yup. I totally understand. I apologize."

I felt like he got it. He got it that I got it. We're probably good now.

"I need you to delete those photos."

"Yup. Right away."

I couldn't believe it, but Carlos had a power over me that I'd never experienced. He was ordering me *over the phone* to delete pictures from my phone and I was 100 percent complying. I wasn't just saying it. I slowed down, opened my photos, and deleted the couple I had taken, just as I was told to.

"Done. Just deleted them. Really sorry about that."

"Please don't do that again, sir."

"Absolutely not. That was a *very* stupid mistake on my part."

"Just be aware that you are now on a list."

You have *to be shitting me.*

"List?"

"It's a potential threat list that all bank security divisions share."

"All Wells Fargos?"

"No. All banks in the United States. You were immediately added when you were seen taking photos today."

"Jesus. How long am I on the list?"

"Indefinitely."

My first thought was regretting that I deleted those photos. I mean, if I'm on a list *indefinitely* I should at least have the evidence on me. But now I had bigger problems. Did the list mean I couldn't have a bank account? I needed to know.

"Can I still bank at that branch?"

"That will be up to them."

The line went dead. Carlos had hung up on me. I was practically shitting myself. I felt like the FBI was going to be waiting for me at the Icehouse. I arrived there about thirty minutes later and, thankfully, they weren't, but Ryan Sickler was.

I told him the whole ordeal: that I'd seen her again, snapped a few photos, and been called by bank security, ordered to delete them, and now I was on a national watch list of potential threats to all banks. Ryan's response:

"You didn't delete the photos of her, did you?"

"Of course I did."

"Why?

"Because Carlos told me to!"

"How's he gonna know what's on your phone?"

"Carlos knows, man! Carlos just knows."

Now I was in a world of shit because Ryan didn't take my word that this woman was hot. I don't remember how I got through my show that night, but the next day I went back to the bank just after they opened.

I asked to speak to the manager. She was a woman in her thirties and, surprisingly, she was very understanding. I told her about the incident before security did.

"They'll probably brief me after lunch."

I asked if I was still allowed to bank there and she said, "Of course." I was so relieved. I felt like I had gone to confession. But there was one thing left to do. I needed to apologize to Natasha.

The manager had her come to the office, and she left me, a potential threat, in there with her all alone. I came clean and told Natasha the whole story. I was so embarrassed by all of it, but you know what she did? She laughed. She thought it was sweet.

"You know, I *am* single."

"Do you want to go out with my friend? This would make *such* a great story."

"You got a picture?" She laughed.

"Actually, I do." I had tons of photos of Ryan. We'd been friends for fifteen years at that point. I took my time. Told her I had to find a good one. I scrolled until I saw one of him smiling. It was taken at a party, and if I were building a dating profile for him, I would have made it his main picture.

She looked for a long beat, considering what to do. Her eyes danced around, her head moved a little, a sway. And then:

"Not my type."

I had to laugh. We parted as friends, and since they both now knew the story, they eventually found each other on Facebook. Ryan called me.

"I shoulda trusted you, man."

"Why's that?"

"Natasha. God *damn*, she looks good."

"I fuckin' told you, man! I'm on a federal watch list because you don't trust your friend."

No Fat Chicks

"No fat chicks."

Phil said this. Phil is a fellow comedian.

He sat across from me at lunch, and my face couldn't hide my bewilderment. I wasn't so taken aback that I lost my ability to speak, but I couldn't hide the emotion on my face, and he saw that. I was looking into Phil's eyes and he knew what I saw: a very large man. He was six foot three and *well* over 300 pounds. You see, Phil was quite fat himself. Some might even say *very* fat. He was smart, witty, and cutting. Phil was extremely opinionated, and that had some appeal, I suppose. He wasn't ugly, but he's the type of guy whom I thought would be thrilled just to have a woman talk to him. But it turns out it was exactly the opposite. Phil was demanding when it came to the opposite sex. Not only did he proclaim "no fat chicks," he also listed other necessities: she needed to "be hot," "make good money," and "not be annoying."

I laughed. A real laugh. I couldn't believe that this tub of shit who had clearly done little to no work on his physical appearance would require a woman who was devoted to hers.

"No fat chicks? Dude, *you're* fat."

"You're fat too."

"We're not talking about me. You're the one saying 'no fat chicks' and you're *very* fat."

He wasn't budging and then he pulled out his phone and showed me something. Photos of a beautiful girl. She *was* hot. I kept swiping photos of her in a bikini, in short shorts, and then it was the two of them together, laughing, *kissing*! Who is she?

"Just some chick I dated for a while. She got annoying."

"You broke up with her?"

"Yup." He just casually let it out like I had asked him, "Do they have paper towels in the bathroom?"

"Yup."

Now I was more intrigued. Phil, the giant turd of a human being who possessed little to no redeeming qualities save for a snarky, sometimes biting sense of humor, had disposed of what would surely be the most attractive woman who would ever come within smelling distance of him because "she got annoying."

"You should really let this woman annoy you. You'll never get anything like this again."

I was serious. I was sure he'd made a grave mistake.

"I'm talking to another chick." He handed me his phone and again, I was blown away. Another stunner. Was he poisoning these women? Why would they go out with Phil? He was doing that shit I'd heard about when I was really young and never took to. He'd even adopted the rallying cry I'd heard countless idiots say.

"Girls like assholes."

It's a philosophy I never really understood. *Girls like assholes.*

What? How does that make any sense? You might be reading this and thinking, *Wait a minute, Tom, you're an asshole.*

I get it. I get that I *can be* an asshole on a mic. Onstage, sure. On the podcast, sometimes. But in real life, I try to keep being an asshole to a minimum. And it was absolutely *never* my approach with women. I should also add that I wasn't the most successful with women, but I was far from a failure. Maybe I should have been an asshole. But I always thought if you like someone, oh, I don't know, try being nice to them?

But here I am looking across the table at "Philly Pig Tits" showing me photos of him with an absolute dime piece. This guy was the biggest oblivious asshole possible, and it was actually working for him.

But it's not just big, fat Phil, is it? Time and time again we see guys who frankly have no business having any standards dating beautiful women. Of course, it's easy to dismiss it as the oldest exchange in the world. Rich man has money, beautiful woman has her beauty; they each have something the other wants. Sure, that dynamic will never end, but that's not what I'm talking about. I'm not talking about rich guys. I'm talking about guys like Phil. They're everywhere. They're fucking entitled, and they have no reason to be. They're just alive. I've met couples like this in all kinds of settings: wedding receptions, dinner parties, house parties, after my shows.

Not-rich Phil-looking motherfucker with a stunning woman. It's made me realize a couple of things:

One, every man in the world can get laid, and I wish they knew it. I really do. Missing a tooth? Have a wound that oozes from your face? It might seem improbable, but there is a woman willing to sleep with you. I am completely convinced of this. It's one of the certainties in this world that has made me completely believe that women are the better species. I'm not saying this to suck up. I'm saying it because it's true, and I wish more men realized that they really do have a shot with a woman. Let me be clear: I'm not saying *every* man has a shot with *every* woman. I'm just saying women forgive a lot more flaws than we do.

Still, I can't stop thinking about what a shitbag Phil is, but when I start to go down that rabbit hole I have to remind myself that I'm not much better than him. He's definitely a bigger dick and grossly entitled, but if I'm being honest with myself I can think of lots of ridiculous reasons I turned down women over the years. I turned down dates and certainly shots at love for the most trivial, bullshit reasons I can think of. For example, one time I didn't like a girl's forehead, so I never called her again. *Her forehead*. It wasn't even a bad one. It's not like it was wide open and bleeding. It was just a little misshapen and shiny. I once turned down a second date with a girl because she said, "Whatever you want" to every question that I asked. I could have given her another try, right? Should I flog myself for that?

This other time, I had a lovely date with a woman, but it never evolved into a relationship. Do you know why? Her feet were too narrow. If you're questioning how that prevented our love from taking off, it's simply because I refused to go out with her again knowing that she had *very* narrow feet. I'm not sure what I thought I needed from her. Wide feet so she could plow through the snow? Some guys don't like fat chicks, and some can't stand narrow feet.

But you know what? Women are just as bad as we are, maybe worse. I discovered that as I was doing research for this essay.

(Yes, I do research.) Every woman I talked to from my sisters to friends to my wife, hell, even the editor of *this book* has stories of their own harsh judgments on us men. They do *exactly* what we do. I was going to conclude this with a big statement about what massive assholes men are, but now I realize we are exactly the same.

My wife went out with a guy but decided his Rocket from the Crypt tattoo was too stupid to take it further.

My sister, Maria, turned down a guy who she said was nice because his eyebrows were trimmed.

My other sister, Jane, thought a guy was "the hottest" she'd ever seen, but he *cuffed his jeans up* in a way she thought was lame.

Another friend stopped seeing a guy because he mispronounced the word "façade." He said, "FUH-KADE."

That was it.

Still another just couldn't tolerate seeing a great guy again because his shoes were *terrible*.

Are you processing this? Here I was, thinking these poor ladies need a break from *us*. I hate to say it, but I think assholes are just what the doctor ordered. These chicks are so full of themselves with their ridiculous standards and preposterous reasons for not giving a guy a shot. They need a reality check, especially the fat ones. Thank God for guys like Phil.

Chris Noth

American 9429, LAX to JFK, 6:53 a.m.

I've never thought about actor Chris Noth more than in the week I turned in this book. It started because the reboot of *Sex and the City* titled *And Just Like That...*(guess they're done with sex?) came out, and he reprised his character, Mr. Big. Apparently, he rides a Peloton in the first episode and dies. People can't stop talking about it, and Peloton did an advertisement with him almost immediately. I didn't even get to see it because just a few days later two women accused him of sexual assault in the past and so Peloton pulled it. I don't know if it's true, and he has publicly denied it, saying they were consensual encounters. At the time of this writing, it's a still-developing story, but here's a different story about the time I flew with him.

By now you've probably noticed the remarkable number of notable black celebrities I've sat next to on flights. You might be wondering, "Do you only fly Soul Plane?" The answer is, "No, but I absolutely would if it were available."

I'm writing about memorable experiences. People and conversations that really stood out. I can shut my eyes and picture myself there. Is it my fault that most of these people are not white? Sure, I flew next to some notable whites. Most of them weren't that exciting or engaging. Christopher Lloyd picked his nose for over two hours. That was pretty cool, I guess. I mean he really dug in there and cleaned it out. It was an excavation. He used the full rotation of his fingers, hands, and arms. Pronation, supination, all of it. I watched for almost the entire duration of the flight. Sometimes I'd go back to reading or watching a movie, and then I'd look back and Lloyd would still be rimming out his nose. It was impressive. Did I want to write a chapter about it here? No. I think the last few sentences were more than enough.

There was one notable white person that I'll never forget sitting next to on a flight and that was Chris Noth. I wasn't yet a ticket seller but I *was* a frequent flier, and that day they called my name at the gate accompanied by the sweetest sentence in the world, "You've been upgraded."

When you're a hustling, grinding, sometimes starving comedian who struggles to pay the bills, there is no better feeling than finding out you're going to fly comfortably for the next few hours. This day it was the *primo* flight from Los Angeles to New York, the big one. Not only is this a long flight, but there's a high probability of notable people on it because it travels between the two cities where the big dawgs live and play.

I was seated first, and a few moments later, Mr. Big of *Sex and the City* fame sat next to me. I immediately recognized him. He's extremely good looking and, of course, famous. Clearly, the women on this flight were *Sex and the City* fans and, *boy*, was it a sight to behold. I've had and have some very good-looking male friends. It's clear when you're with them that they have an effect on the opposite sex. Women look at them in a way they've never looked at me. They linger and laugh when nothing funny is said. It stands out to you as a guy because you realize it's the way *you* act toward beautiful women. It's fascinating, a little embarrassing, and hilarious to watch. I've been around these guys, but *this* was Mr. Big. This reached a whole other level. Mouths dropped, drool formed. The young, very attractive flight attendant serving us was trembling, literally. She "forgot" to ask me what I wanted to drink and brought him a coffee that must have been terrible. He cringed.

"Jesus *Christ*! This is the worst coffee I've ever had."

He wasn't being an asshole. He was having a terrible coffee experience. I can respect that.

He called another flight attendant over and handed her the coffee, explaining that it was bad, really bad. We began a conversation, and I have to say, when you start talking to someone famous, you have expectations. Well, at least I do. I never know if this person will be open, pretentious, engaging, or aloof. But Chris Noth was pretty damn awesome. He was curious and generous with stories, a natural conversationalist—the type of person I'd later learn is great to have on a podcast. When the young flight attendant returned with the new coffee, she was staring at him, frozen, as if she was unsure how to speak. His response: "Oh, come on! It's a *show*!" I know what you're thinking, but from my perspective it was an understandable reaction; and it was genuine, it just spilled out of him.

Dude was *totally* over it. It got me thinking how exhausting it must be if all day, every day, women in this country fixated on you, living out a fantasy from a TV show where you played a part as an actor. Fun for a while, I'm sure. But after a few *years* of it? That has to be taxing, especially if you love the craft of acting. And, sure, maybe you're having sex with some of them, but after a few thousand it's gotta get old, right? Not that I'm saying that Chris Noth was having sex with thousands of his fans, but if he was, God bless.

I went up to use the bathroom and caught the older flight attendant actually lecturing the younger one.

"Keep it together. He's just another passenger."

Holy shit! I'd never seen anything like this before; a woman was physically falling apart, incapable of doing her work because of a guy's presence. It was like those videos you'd see of Michael Jackson and other pop stars visiting Eastern European countries who weren't used to being in the presence of celebrities. People would weep and faint. This was incredible! I guess I didn't really believe stuff like this happened in real life. When I returned to my seat I told Chris Noth about it, but I did not get the reaction I expected.

He shook his head.

"Goddammit." He was totally resigned. I realized it had to be the hundred thousandth time he'd heard something like this. I took it as a cue to change the topic.

"*Law and Order* is great!" At the time he was only a few years removed from *Law & Order,* but that show was replayed on so many different channels you'd swear he was still on set.

"Procedural."

I didn't even know what he meant by it, but I nodded. I knew "procedural" was shorthand for crime shows like *Law & Order* and *CSI.* Those shows follow the format where a crime is committed, investigated, and solved, all in one episode. I thought he was down on himself about being a part of that show, so I tried to lift him up.

"Those shows are so good."

"I'm thankful because it's given me financial security, but as an actor there's nothing to it. It's just the same thing over and over."

I thought about it. He's right. Those shows really do follow a blueprint that never seems to change.

The detective asks the cabdriver, "Did you notice anything odd about the guy you picked up on Saturday night? Would have been after midnight." And the cabdriver never even flinches, like he gets questioned by detectives every few days. The actors playing detectives also squint a lot. It's apparently a job requirement to have a solid squint face when playing a detective on television. If you went to drama school I'm sure you want to flex more than your eyelids. Most people say, "Who cares? Do you know how much money these actors make?" True, but while getting paid well is nice, it can't be all that fulfilling as an actor.

I'd never really considered that someone on a hit show might be yearning for something more. As I contemplated what he'd said, he interjected. "You know what's great, though? Who is doing great work with the writing and, oh my god, the acting!"

I had no idea what he was going to say, but I *really* wasn't expecting what he said next.

"*Downton Abbey.*"

Huh?

"Really?"

"The stories! And what those actors are doing...best show on television."

He was so animated about it—I could tell he was yearning to

do that type of work, but also he clearly *loved* the show. I have to say it did stick with me, and not long afterward, I watched *Downton Abbey*. All of it. Including the specials. And the movie. It's epic and absolutely a masterpiece. I never imagined that I—a dirty comic who talks about sex and race and the general nonsense that I encounter—would become totally invested in what happened between the Crawleys and their servants. The stories, the drama, the acting! Chris Noth couldn't have been more right. Lady Mary and the Turk! Lord Grantham's financial distress! What has Bates done?! I can't wait for the Dowager's next quip!

I was reminded of something I once heard that I wish I could attribute to the correct source, but I have no idea who said it. "When it comes to art, greatness is not subjective. Greatness is undeniable." Kudos for the rec, Chris Noth. You're the only worthwhile white I've ever flown with.

I really hope the accusations against Noth aren't true. If you can't trust someone who recommends *Downton Abbey* to be a good person, who *can* you trust in this world?

What's the Theme?

Just when you think you have it figured out, it'll change on you. Just when you think you know how it works, it doesn't.

I am, of course, a fan of comedy. I love comedy and comedians. Even after all these years. It can take more to make me laugh, and I know what sucks and *why* it sucks more than your average person, but watching great stand-up live or a great special is still one of the best feelings—it's art. (Side note: Nothing is as deflating as hearing someone you like or your friends or family praise mediocre comedy or a comedian you don't like. You feel a little piece of you die when it happens.

"You know that *Clark Doreshin* is such a funny guy!"

dying inside

"Yeah, he's uh, definitely got something about him. Very funny."

"Have you heard his joke about hairspray? It's like it should be called *Facespray* because your whole face gets sprayed!"

"That *is* funny."

You have to let it go and remind yourself that they don't know any better and you have to let people like what they like, but still, it's the absolute worst. If that sounds petty, it is. Comedy cliques are like middle school.)

A one-hour special is the cornerstone of achievement for any stand-up comic, and in 2012 I wanted to get my own. Comedy specials are how I discovered stand-up. When I first saw Eddie Murphy's *Delirious* I laughed harder than I ever had in my life at that point. His swagger, his total command of the stage, the voices, the characters, ice cream! Eddie was an introduction to what was *really* funny. There was the funny you had experienced in your life thus far and then there was Eddie. I didn't know a human being was capable of this level of hilarity. In a similar way, seeing Chris Rock perform *Bring the Pain* was a total revelation. Never before had I been so mesmerized for an entire hour. This was a different kind of funny, it was *punching* you in the face. It was fearless and smart. His bit about needing *bullet control* instead of gun control was an undeniable work of art. And Louis CK's *Shameless* was effortlessly hilarious and honest. He articulated observations that I'd never heard in stand-up before, like hating a friend who has dumb questions like "What would you do if you had a time machine?" And the way he broke down "suck a bag of dicks" with genuine curiosity made me realize how genuinely examining even a crude insult can result in hilarity.

I had been a comedian for ten years in 2012. I had worked my way from being an MC who greets audiences as they order wings and beers to a "feature" act who does twenty minutes of material to warm up the crowd for the headliner to becoming a headliner myself. I was at the place I wanted to be, but there was one big problem. Even though I could perform an hour of material and kill, I couldn't get anyone to buy a ticket to see me do it. Nobody knew who I was. I *needed* an hour special, and I needed it to air on a big platform so people could see my special, love it, and then *buy* tickets to see me perform. I told my manager at the time that I was ready for this. He made some calls but soon came back to me with a disappointing answer: Not now. The big players at the time, mainly Comedy Central, signaled that *maybe* later was an option. I didn't feel like waiting, so I did what I would have told another comic to do: Do it yourself.

I hired an audio engineer, and I recorded an album on my own called *White Girls with Cornrows*. The title was based on a bit in the hour about knowing you are in a terrible neighborhood if you see a white girl with cornrows. If you see one, you can be sure she is down for *whatever*. Of course, this wasn't the hour special that I was really hoping to do, but still, an audio-only recording of this material could reach a bigger audience than me touring and performing for people who were getting free tickets. It wouldn't air on Comedy Central or HBO, but I could sell the CD at shows and I'd own the audio rights, so when Sirius XM or Pandora played a track, that $0.000023 generated was coming back to Papa.

I recorded my album at the Comedy Works South club in Denver. That's the bigger of the two venues in Denver, but also the less desirable one. I wanted to record at the downtown location because that's the club where all the comics love to perform, and with good reason. Comedy Works Downtown is like a cheat code for doing stand-up and it's hard to explain why, but essentially, it's the *perfect* comedy club. You go downstairs into a dark performance space with tight, low ceilings. You can *pack* the room with people so there's maybe 280 bodies in there with not a lot of room for much else. The sound when you are killing is deafening. But the most impressive thing about it is it's also the club where one of the greatest albums of all time was recorded: *Skanks for the Memories* by Dave Attell.

You become a fan of different comedians at different points in your life. I had gone through my Cosby into Murphy into Carlin and Def Jam phases, and by my early days as a stand-up I was at Attell. I was a latecomer to Attell's comedy, but I fell in love with his work right away, and it was *Skanks for the Memories* that completely changed the way I thought about doing stand-up. Attell was all about the *jokes*.

Isn't every comic all about the jokes?

No.

Comics care about different things. The *message* is important to some, the *truth* is what matters to others, *raw vulnerability* is at the top of some comics' lists, but Dave put all that aside. His motivation was simple: What's the funniest thing I can say about this? That's all that matters.

Watching Attell work was always a treat. He would have crowds in the palm of his hand, and he did it in a way that I completely fell in love with. First, when he arrived at the club he would talk to the staff at the club like he was there delivering beer. He had this salt-of-the-earth quality that made me realize that a big-time act could actually behave that way: personable and accessible. He didn't have any aloofness or arrogance to him. He talked to audience members so casually during a show, and he'd go from whatever he had asked them into an off-the-cuff hilarious comment, then into a masterfully crafted joke. It was incredible to watch. He took risks too. He'd do a joke on Thursday that killed, and then on Friday he'd try a different line instead of the punch line that already worked, then Saturday instead of going back to the proven line, he'd try yet another. It was inspiring. That might be hard to believe about a guy who can do thirty minutes on anal beads, but it's true. And while we're on the topic of anal beads, I'm here to say that dirty jokes aren't lesser jokes. The notion that dirty makes it easy is nonsense. Go watch an amateur comedian tell "jokes" about blow jobs and sex and you will *cringe* at how badly it goes. That's because simply being dirty isn't enough. You have to *craft the joke* to make it funny.

There's a danger when you become a huge fan of another comedian while you're still young and honing your own act: You try to incorporate some of their techniques, but you end up just doing a shitty impression. I've seen it many times over the years, but looking back at yourself doing it is harder. First, I copied Chris Rock's stage persona, and now I'd moved on to copying

Me doing my best Attell.

Dave Attell's cadence, pacing, and I was even dressing like him! Yes, for a few years I looked like I was living by an underpass writing a manifesto.

So I wanted to record my album at the Comedy Works Downtown location because it's the better club for audiences (Downtown brings the young people, South club brings the suburban types) but also because it's where Attell recorded his. But the club didn't make it available to me. I just wasn't big enough of an act. So I accepted the offer to play at the South club, and I did the recording there.

I hired a photographer I knew from the improv clubs to do the cover and graphics and *boom*—I had an album. A few major companies approached me about releasing it and distributing it through their shiny corporate labels, but I declined their offers. I wanted to release it myself. I figured if I had done all the work already, why chop it up with someone who is just going to put it on sites where you can sell or stream it? The technology had evolved to the point where we, the comedians, could do that ourselves. So I found a website called CD Baby that was actually developed for musicians, and I posted *White Girls with Cornrows* there. The site made your album available for purchase on all the big sites like iTunes and Amazon and allowed you to have physical copies manufactured as well. I clicked a button and *ding ding ding*—I had put out my own album. Something I had written, performed, and now owned. I wouldn't have to split any part of it with a corporation, just a small fee with CD Baby. I was able to earn enough where I could move and pay bills for a while. It also gave me monthly deposits in amounts of money I had never seen at that point.

I always encourage comics to take this route and love seeing when they take it upon themselves to get their material out. We live in a time where you no longer need permission to be creative. You can actually do it all yourself. You should.

The next year, I got the opportunity I had been waiting for, praying for, pacing for: to do a one-hour special.

The path to getting it was different than I had imagined. See, in 2010, I was lucky enough to do a *half*-hour special on Comedy Central after my third year submitting. The long-running series was called *Comedy Central Presents*. Some of my favorite comics ever had a *Presents*, and when I got the call that I'd be doing one, I thought life couldn't be better. I was following in the right footsteps.

I remember the day I recorded it, one of producers pulled me into a dressing room and said, almost as if it were something they could foresee, "This is going to change your road business," meaning, "You're going to start selling tickets now." I felt a surge

The night I filmed a Presents in 2010 with Matt Fulchiron, Kyle Kinane, and Jay Larson, who all shot that night as well.

of adrenaline. I knew not to tell anyone, but I was secretly beaming. It was as if I had auditioned and was told, "Don't tell anyone, but the director loves you."

Your road business changing is *exactly* what every comedian wants. Comedians want to be able to do shows and *sell* tickets. They want to perform for people who *want* to be at that show and who know they're going to see a specific person, you know, a fan. That's an important distinction, because all of us do shows for a long time for people who don't necessarily know *who* they're going to see perform. Before people know who you are in the world of stand-up, you perform to crowds who get *free* tickets. That's right—*free 99 is the price.* How does that work for a business like a comedy club? It's simple. Comedy clubs hire not-yet-famous comedians and pay them a small fee. The club "papers" or gives away free tickets to hundreds of customers who then watch a show for *free* but have a "two-item minimum." The customer *must* order at least two items: burgers, nachos, beers. That's where the money *really* is for the clubs: in the food and beverage. For a comic, those shows are tough but necessary. You learn how to be a real pro, and you end up eating shit a number of times along the way.

I have had world-class bombs. I had a table of twelve leave when there were only fifteen people in the audience. I don't remember how our disagreement started, but I do remember calling a woman at the table a cunt, and that was over pretty quickly.

I was disinvited to a golf outing the day after a *charity show* I was asked to perform at for Carson Palmer, who at the time was the quarterback for the Cincinnati Bengals. My set had been chaotic. Of the 150 or so people in the room who were all standing and talking to one another *before* my set started, about six stopped to watch me perform. The rest just continued mingling as if I were a public service announcer letting them know about the parking situation. I ended up finding a younger kid in the crowd, and I talked to him directly since no one else would listen. I told him I was Brett Favre and he believed me. I told him the key to my success was eating ass at a young age. Show. Over. No golf either.

I was booed offstage at a comedy club in Winnipeg. It was a sold-out Saturday night, the early show. I had just taken the stage after the middle act, a Black Canadian comic, had a great set, like he'd had all week. Nothing signaled to me that anything was going to go south. But a few minutes into my set I heard a guy two tables from the stage speaking loudly. I called him out and he replied sincerely that he was talking about his dog. He literally said, "I'm talking about my dog."

Oh, that's nice.

It was odd that he would share that, since it was obvious that a show was going on. I responded the way I think a comic should, by insulting him.

"You should think about putting your face in a bowl like a dog does because none of us want to hear you talk."

What I didn't realize at that moment is that the guy wasn't just there with the people at his table. I mean if they got mad, who cares? It's four people. They can leave. He was there with a group of eighty. This was their holiday outing. When I told one of their own to eat out of a bowl like a dog, they took it as an insult to all of them. The booing started and it grew. Twenty minutes later they were shouting, "Bring back the Black guy!" And soon I obliged.

No wonder the Jets, their NHL hockey team, had left the city in 1996, I thought.

I told them they were the worst and I brought him back onstage.

All these disasters had one thing in common: The audience had free entry to the show.

Selling tickets is by far the hardest thing to do on the business side of stand-up comedy, so I needed something that would change my road work.

My half-hour special was the first to come out, in January of 2011, and the effect was amazing—and by that I mean it did absolutely nothing. I should point out that it was a *well-received* half hour. Comics and industry people all gave me props. People *seemed* to dig it. There was only one problem: It didn't help me sell one more ticket. If it did, it certainly wasn't notable. Clubs didn't really give a shit that I had a *Presents*, and it was just like, well, nothing had happened. When people say, "Why is so and so who is funny and has a funny special not selling tickets?" I've come to a conclusion:

I don't know.

Neither do you and neither does anyone else. Everyone has theories but none of us know anything. Why was *Big Bang Theory* a bona fide megahit? Why isn't Geoff Tate doing arenas? I don't know. People say it's luck, circumstance, talent, timing. It's all of that, maybe?

In 2013, my manager called me and said, "Let's run your hour and invite people to come and see it." Meaning: networks. Meaning, most importantly, Comedy Central. Comedy Central was the mountaintop outside of HBO, which was just completely unapproachable because HBO was reserved for only superstars. Chris Rock. George Carlin. Robin Williams. You had to be an absolute megastar to be on HBO, but Comedy Central seemed attainable and, again, it's where so many comics I looked up to had a home. I had already been on the network a few times doing shorter sets and then, of course, my half hour. In my mind there was no better place to be, and I didn't have much doubt this was just ceremonial. I was going to be doing my first hour on Comedy Central. I set up a special night at Flappers in Burbank where I had offered tickets to anybody who wanted to see the show on my podcast.

We actually got hundreds of replies. People were willing to come and watch the show and be a great audience for my set. I ran the set and felt really great about it. The crowd was incredible and I knew I had nailed it. In spite of all that, the feedback I got from the network was, "What's the theme? There doesn't seem to be a theme."

Huh?

That's what I was told Comedy Central's feedback was. "What's the theme?"

"The theme is *funny jokes*."

"I know. Yeah, that's what they're saying."

"Well, what the fuck, man? Does there have to be a throughline to this? Like there has to be something that carries from beginning to end? What am I, fucking British?"

That was that. That's how I found out I wouldn't be doing an hour special on Comedy Central. My manager had told me they were looking for a theme. In retrospect, they just didn't want it. At least, some executive who never wrote or performed comedy but somehow was given the task of selecting who is worthy of a large platform didn't want it.

That was it. That was my dream, and it was over, and I didn't know what to do.

Then I got the call that a company named Comedy Dynamics was willing to shoot it on spec, meaning they would take the risk and incur the cost of shooting the special. They would give me a small fee and a percentage of ownership, and then they would be able to license and sell the special. It didn't just feel like a consolation prize, it *was* one. But it was the only one I was getting so I said, "Yes."

In November of 2013, I shot *Completely Normal*, my first one-hour special. I chose to shoot it in Minneapolis because it had always been a great comedy city to me in the times that I had been there before. A couple months later—after the horrific process of watching myself, and editing, and color correcting, and mixing—I got a phone call while I was driving up La Cienega and I pulled over. My manager at the time told me, "You have an offer." I got excited. Comedy Central must have seen the special and realized they should have made it. I braced myself for a triumphant moment.

"Comedy Central passed."

Fuck. *Really?*

I said, "Dude, they already said no."

"I know, but this time we sent them the special and they passed again."

You know how that girl said she didn't like you? I called her for you and she said she still doesn't like you.

"Why are you telling me? I only knew that they had said 'no' once and that was enough. You're double confirming the 'no'?"

Then he said, "HBO passed."

"We sent it to HBO?"

"Yeah, we sent it to everyone."

I was legitimately excited that someone at HBO had even *seen* it.

"Well, you have an offer." My heart was racing, my breath got short. I needed to compose myself.

"Where?"

"Netflix."

"Netflix?"

It might sound crazy as you read this, but it was not the same as getting that phone call now. Netflix had just started coming out of their business of mailing DVDs to consumers and was trying this new "streaming" thing. It was definitely a letdown.

My manager could sense it.

"Yeah, you know, they keep growing. They have like forty million subscribers now."

"Oh, okay. That's . . . good."

He goes, "Yeah, that's almost as many as HBO. And you know, Burr has one on there. It's doing really well for him, so I think it's a pretty good opportunity." And I said, "Well, then I'm happy to be there. I mean, yeah, let's go to Netflix. Too bad it's not Comedy Central."

A few months later, in March of 2014, my special debuted. And after a week or so, I honestly didn't think much more was going to happen than some tweets and some comments. Just like a few years before when I had done my half-hour special. A couple people stopped me on the street. But something happened in June. I was working the Cleveland Improv, and after the weekend, the manager came up to me with his paperwork of my ticket sales from the weekend. I remember like it was yesterday. He said, "I don't know what the hell happened, but you hit some bonuses this weekend." I didn't really get what he was trying to say. He looked at me incredulously. "People bought tickets to see you, but I don't know why they'd do that." He was *such* an asshole, but he was right. It didn't even register to me that it had anything to do with the special.

As the year went on, it was happening more and more, and by the end of the year, I was selling out clubs and adding shows. Finally, I was selling tickets.

Sincerity is frowned upon from comedians. I get it. People turn to us for jokes, for laughter. Even and especially *other* comedians will give you a hard time for being sincere. They'll mock you, often in hilarious fashion, for expressing anything from the heart. I told a struggling comedian friend I'd do "anything" for him because I would. I know some of the tough times he's been through. When I said it, I meant it. He looked at me like he was going to cry and then he took a beat, unzipped his pants, and stared at me. It was funny and, no, I didn't touch his penis. But that is why I'm prefacing the following by stating that I want to be sincere here. I promise that the following sentences are not a joke. I especially want to say this to artists: I'm improbably successful in the comedy world. You don't know the full scope of it, but it's almost unimaginable. I'm not telling you that to brag. I'm saying it because I'm really not *special*. I wasn't *chosen*, and I didn't have a team of tastemakers behind me making my dreams happen. I made them happen, and you can make yours happen too. I mean it. If you're a comedian, writer, actor, painter, director, dancer, or any other type of artist, you can make your dreams happen. You can have the career and the life that you dream of. The only thing I did was believe I could do it, and I took action. You *must* do the same. You have to know you are meant to do your craft and you have to act. You have to write, dance, paint, get onstage, express yourself however you feel compelled to, and you have to take a chance *on yourself.* I recorded my own album, submitted for what was available, and started my own podcast. I'm not special, but I didn't wait for something to happen. I took calculated risks, and you can and should do the same. Make the life you want happen for yourself because you really can.

Trickin' on the Track

When I arrived in LA, I wasn't a touring comedian yet. I was dreaming of becoming one, but dreams don't pay shit, so I needed an actual job. I saw an ad asking for people willing to be "spa attendants" and I went for it. I always liked spas and didn't mind the idea of folding towels at one while helping someone unwind from their hectic life. I imagined my days would be filled with the smell of eucalyptus and the sight of totally relaxed customers walking in robes and sandals from one treatment room to the next. This spa was called Splash—The Relaxation Spa. It didn't take long to figure out that "Splash" wasn't a spa. It was an hourly rental hot tub fuck spot. Rooms were given names like Barcelona or Japanese Garden with poorly thrown-together decorations to fit the theme. The Japanese Garden had a cheap fountain and some plastic plants so you might *lose yourself* in the illusion they'd created. You paid $100 an hour to use the rooms, which really means to fuck in them. That's what people did. They either arrived with someone to fuck there or they'd meet someone there and then fuck them. And I cleaned it up. It was so awkward, but also exciting to watch people meet up who had only spoken on the phone. I love people-watching, and this felt like a bonus level. Most of the customers weren't going on romantic dates, which is how Splash advertised their business.

"Looking for a fun thing to do on date night? Try Splash!"

The owner made it clear that he didn't want people to think his place was a jizz factory, but that's clearly what it was. *Most* people were going there for sex with people they had yet to meet.

It was almost like the time I was walking on Sunset Boulevard late and a car pulled over, rolled down the window, and a man asked me, "How much?" That's right, yours truly was mistaken for walking the ho stroll. Sunset west of Fairfax, east of Crescent was and perhaps still is an active prostitution area aka a "track." That is, of course, a track of your standard hoes. Females and sometimes the occasional male ho. There's a very popular stretch on Santa Monica Boulevard of transsexual prostitutes. I know this because I lived on Mansfield, between Fountain and Santa Monica, when I first moved to Los Angeles. I'm only pointing this out so if you visit Los Angeles and you're wondering which area to go to, well, what's your preference? It was a dicey neighborhood to say the least.

I saw celebrities park their cars, get drugs and hoes, and then go back to their cars and leave. I'm talking A-list here, super famous. I'd just sit on the balcony and watch.

The Spa was a different story. I didn't even realize what it was for a few days. I was twenty-two and had never been to or even heard of a place like this. The occasional couple did come in. It made sense to see this as an option to spice things up in a relationship, but the majority of people going there were just meeting up for sex that they paid for. See, the owner had one rule above all else—the entire party must be present before they enter a room. Like restaurants that won't seat you until everyone is present. Only the spa rules actually made sense. If someone showed up, went to the room, and waited for the other person to show up, they could say their "time" didn't start until the other person arrived. The owner didn't like that, so he made it a rule. You enter the room together and that's when the time starts. That rule led to a *lot* of super uncomfortable dudes in the lobby. I mean, pacing, sweating, and flat-out panicking. I'd stand there almost feeling for them, the anticipation building to a fever pitch, waiting for the door to open and their "date" to enter.

Sometimes she was an absolute smoke show, others she wasn't so hot. One time a guy nervously paced back and forth, and then two guys walked in. One of them said, "Erik?" and then Erik(?) said, "Mario?" and then Erik and Mario and friend went into the Barcelona Room and three minutes later they all left. I went in the room thinking they had changed their minds, but wouldn't you know it—there were three used condoms just lying there. Love connection?

I'm most surprised that more customers at this establishment weren't alarmed by me and more specifically my face. I have been, for years, labeled by strangers as a cop or "looking like a cop." It's not a compliment. It started early. When I moved during my freshman year in high school from the suburbs of Milwaukee to Vero Beach, I did what most new kids would do at a new school— I asked who had drugs and where the party would be that weekend. I got blank stares until one kid asked me a question.

"How old are you?"

"Fourteen."

"Really? You look older."

"Yeah I guess so, but yeah, I'm fourteen."

He rolled his eyes and walked away. It took months of not getting straight answers before someone who I befriended told me, "Everyone thought you were a narc."

As a freshman in college I really did look older. Like, I looked thirty. This time I used it to my advantage. On the first day of school in the freshman dorms I walked down the hall, and two guys who had their door open flinched when I walked by. I immediately turned around and walked into their room.

"Where is it, guys?"

They were busted and quickly gave up their twelve-pack.

"Come on. You know the rules."

I had just become a corrupt cop, and it felt great. A few years later after my time at Splash I was working a restaurant job in Los Angeles on Sunset Boulevard. It had some questionable types that would stop in, but of course we took care of them because hoes gotta eat too. One of the guys that hung with the working girls ordered, and when I walked out to bring him his food he said in a very clear and distinct voice, "Thank you, Officer."

I stopped.

"What?"

"Nothing." He sipped from his lemonade. I turned back and walked away.

"Officer." He muttered it again.

I kept walking. Pissed. I went inside and told my coworker, Todd, what had just happened. I felt so slighted. His eyes widened and his face lit up.

"Bro! You look *just* like a cop!"

"I don't see it."

Omarion

Delta 2601, MCO to LAX, 12:17 p.m.

Some of these can be hard to believe. I get it. I'm making claims. I'm telling stories about famous people, and you just have to... what? Believe it? Well, you don't. I have photographic evidence of a lot of them.

This one here, you can't really tell, but that's Omarion—the R & B singer. I'm sitting right next to him. That's him in the aisle seat. I know it just looks like a guy with a blanket over his head, but that's what he did. We sat down and he put a blanket over his head. And he slept like that for the entire flight from Orlando to Los Angeles. I remember thinking, *This is a clinically insane person.* In retrospect, I really respect it. I'm a big, *big* fan of blackout curtains. What is better than sleeping in a pitch-black room? Well, that would be a *cold*, pitch-black room. I could sleep through the winter if no one would wake me. And yeah, a sleep mask is ideal in these situations, but if you don't have one—improvise. Put a blanket over your head and check out. Big props to "O."

I'll be honest, I didn't know that was Omarion, but a couple other people did. And then, when we had landed in LA, he did something I had never seen anybody do. As soon as we stepped off the plane and onto the jet bridge, he took a hoverboard out of his backpack and rode it up the jet bridge and through the airport to baggage claim. For real. It was the smoothest shit I've ever seen. It was one of the first ones I had ever seen—no, it might have actually been *the* first one I ever saw. I wasn't entirely sure what was happening.

Is that dude floating with that? I need to get one of those... There's no way I can afford one.

And he was an expert. No shaking or nervousness. He didn't even need a moment to stabilize himself on it. He just put it down, stepped on, and went. It's like he invented the hoverboard. (He didn't. That was Shane Chen.) It was one of the slickest, most baller moves I'd ever witnessed, and I would try to do the same if I wasn't 100 percent certain that I would suffer life-altering injuries within seconds of stepping on one.

Pick One

When you're a kid and you have siblings it's common to wonder, "Do my parents love one of us more than the other?" My sisters and I would ask that a lot, and my parents would always say the same thing: "We love you all the same. You'll understand one day. Parents don't love one kid more than the other."

Now as a father myself I know that isn't entirely true. I always love whichever kid isn't crying or whining more than the one who is, but still, that feels temporary. Even though I'm a grown-ass man with children of my own, I still wonder the same thing with my own parents. The difference is that any time I asked my dad that same question in the last couple years, he didn't hesitate. "You're my favorite."

Damn, that feels good.

"What about you, Mom?"

"I love Jane the most because she loves me the most."

Uh, okay. I guess that's good news for Jane and me and not so great for Maria, my older sister.

I have two sons. I adore them both equally. As of this writing my oldest boy, Ellis, just turned six. My youngest, Julian, is three. They couldn't be more different. I'll begin with demeanor. The three-year-old is easygoing. He laughs a lot and listens when you say something *twice*. Ellis doesn't really play that shit. He wants what he wants and *fuck you* if you don't go along with him. I thought it was our parenting or discipline, but then I realized that's just him. The modern, evolved parent would say he's "decisive" and even "stubborn." But I'll be honest, he's kind of a *dick*. That isn't to say he's not a sweet boy, because he is. He *can* be. He can also be a real dick. At least he's funny.

He's really into snakes right now. He has stuffed animal snakes, he talks about snakes, and he wants to do nothing more than watch snake videos all day.

When I say "snake videos" I don't mean a video of a snake just moving around or resting in a cave. He likes watching them hunt and eat. Because of him, I've seen them all. And, if you're wondering, YouTube is to blame. The first time I searched "snakes" on that platform it was just an animal expert showing you a snake. Then I felt the need to show him that snakes can bite and some are venomous. I showed him that video so he wouldn't think he could just walk up to a snake and pick it up. Soon after, we were watching snakes eat *everything*. Snakes eating mice, rabbits, lizards, pigs, cows, you name it. The first ten times I stopped playing them a few seconds after they started.

"I don't think you want to see that, buddy."

"I do, I do. I want to see him eat it."

"Are you sure? That's pretty intense."

And I swear to you, with a gleeful smile he pronounced, "I do! I like it."

Whoa.

I mean, I've watched all the serial killer shows and biographies, and I feel like this part is familiar. He's not hurting animals but he sure doesn't mind watching nature take its course. I feel like these videos would be a lot even for adults to handle, but it's oddly soothing for my six-year-old.

Ellis is more physical and risk-taking by nature than his brother. When he approaches the end of a platform he looks down and then just jumps. Julian looks, assesses, and then decides, "That might be too far to jump."

Verbally, it's kind of astonishing. I have learned that it's common for the second child to progress more rapidly than the first due to the fact that the second child is greatly influenced by their older sibling whom they spend a great deal of time with. It makes sense. Your second kid is around your first kid all day. The second kid has someone to model after, to learn how to move, how to speak, how to exist in this world.

The three-year-old was speaking in complicated, complete sentences at eighteen months and doing so while correctly conjugating verbs.

While he speaks well, we've had the recent development of Julian not liking his own name, which is fun. We found out because he yelled at us one day when we called him by his name, as we have done since we named him. We have nicknames for him, like Julián but with a Spanish pronunciation like WHO-LEE-YAWN. Sometimes we call him Jujito or Juju. He was all about those names until about three months ago when, out of nowhere, he rejected all of his names and started naming himself. First he said his name was Beeshu. I asked him where he got that name, and he simply replied, "California."

Makes sense, I thought.

But they've kept coming at an alarming pace. If you even *try* to call him Julian, he gets *very* upset.

"I'm not Julian!"

Some of his self-proclaimed names that we've all had to adhere to at home lately are: Moth, Mr. Dog, Mr. Parking Lot, Window, Mr. President, Blender, Steppin' Stone, and Red Light, Green Light, Yellow Light. And, yes, you *must* name all three lights or he doesn't acknowledge you.

It's been an interesting challenge, and I must say when he insists on not responding to his given name he quickly becomes my *not* favorite son.

Ellis took longer with his language development. He understood a lot but spoke in two-, three-, and four-word sentences, many times grammatically incorrect. He was saying things like "I do," "Give me more," and "I hold you," which was a misspoken attempt at saying, "Hold me." I knew the big sentences were coming soon. I would always get really excited when he spoke. It wasn't just that he had this adorable little voice. I was bracing myself with anticipation for what would be his first complete sentence of more than a few words to me. He clearly understood pretty complicated language structure himself and he was giving all signs that he was processing what was said. If we discussed that we would go swimming after we ran errands and did some work, he would interject.

"No. Now!"

He understood and he knew what he wanted to say, he just needed a little time to express it fully.

The short sentences continued until the magical day when my firstborn son spoke his first full sentence to his father.

I remember it so clearly. I had gone from the kitchen to the play area where he was sitting by himself, surrounded by toys, drawing on a piece of paper with a crayon. I greeted him the same way my father had greeted me my whole life.

"Hey, buddy! What ya doing?"

I sat down next to him ready to enjoy a few moments with my toddler. That was when he looked directly into my eyes and said it.

"I'd like to play alone, please."

Holy shit. There it is. I smiled, convinced it was said in jest. And the look on his face told me it was not. He stared at me longer than you would if you're joking. It was the kind of look someone would give you if they were on the phone and needed you to leave. You know exactly what their look is saying.

Get out.

I had to respect it. Not only was it his wish, it was also a credo I deeply believe in. I love to play alone. I would take it further and say that I *need* to be alone. Not all the time, of course. I'm not a recluse. I actually love being around people, until I don't. The perfect social setting for me is being surrounded by people I care about and love, and not too many of them. I love a small hang. But I need to be able to say, "I gotta go," sometimes without warning when I need some time to myself. It's just the way I am. Luckily for me, I have built an ecosystem around myself that supports this. All my good friends know that every once in a while I'm going to need to go do some shit by myself and it doesn't mean I don't love them. Some days I don't want to see anyone, and I savor the time to just exist. I don't want you to think I'm building bombs in a cabin with no power. I don't like being *that* alone. I just like some space from time to time. My parents know it, my siblings know it, my wife knows it, and now you know it too. We can definitely be friends, but when I need some space you're going to have to give it to me. If you don't, well, we're not going to be friends. It's nothing new. When I was a kid I could occupy myself for *hours* simply by playing with cars. To this day, my parents rave about how easy I was at that age, compared to my sisters, who needed more attention. It feels like they're saying, "Thank God we could ignore you," but I get it.

My son's language has exploded since that first complete sentence. I mean, he's six now, so this would be a different chapter if it never had.

The Last Time My Son Spoke does sound like a nice title.

He still often tells me he wants to be alone, only now it's usually far less politely. "Go away!" "Get out of here!" "Fuckin' leave!" Which I do not approve of a six-year-old telling his father. I immediately correct him, "That's not okay to say. Only grown-ups can talk like that." But when I walk away I usually smile and laugh. It's such a trip to see your kid not just speaking the way you speak, but also feeling the way you feel. When he says these things to me, my eyes widen and I feel his sentiment in a way that nothing else makes me feel. It feels like we are connected, like I'm seeing what DNA can do in a way that eye color and height can't make you feel. It's moments like those where I realize this really is a little version of me, and then I say to myself, "This is my favorite son."

For now.

What's Wrong with Me?

As I sat across from Dr. Drew Pinsky, the renowned addiction specialist and broadcaster, I beamed. I always get a little extra boost of excitement when I know I'll be sharing what I consider to be my prized possessions: a collection of absurd video clips from the web. On my long-running podcast, *Your Mom's House*, we specialize in finding and sharing the most outrageous clips the internet has to offer. The more inappropriate, disgusting, and disturbing, the better. Our guests sit in a chair facing a monitor, and the podcast shifts between interview, conversation, and showcasing our clips. The goal is always to get the guest to laugh or cry watching what we show them. Most of the time we have comedians on, so having someone as educated, articulate, and frankly put together as Dr. Drew was a new world for us. I could only fantasize about what he would say. He always had fantastic insight whenever I had seen him react on other shows. But those other shows weren't going to show him what we had. We had videos that made people shut off their phones. Would he laugh, scream, walk out? The anticipation and exhilaration were killing me.

I never imagined I would have a podcast. In 2009, my friend

Joe Rogan began doing one out of his house. He would invite friends over and we would sit on a couch in his office and chat. I thought he was kind of crazy for doing it, but this is the same guy who talked about his sensory deprivation tank, so I thought, *This is just another weird thing he's into.* He kept telling me to do one, and I kept shrugging it off. In 2010 on a random weeknight my phone rang, and it was Joe.

"Dude, I saw your wife at the Improv. She's hilarious."

"Yeah, she is."

"You *have* to do a podcast together."

And so in late 2010 we began what would become one of the biggest comedy podcasts. When we started, we would go over to Brian Redban's (Joe's producer at the time) apartment in Burbank to record the first forty episodes. We had no idea what to do, so we just...talked. We would have the same conversations we were having at home, only now they were on mic. Soon we discovered that people were actually listening and the show began to expand. We went from simple conversations to interviewing comics, then building segments and ultimately, my favorite, playing clips. Clips have become a staple of the podcast along with almost always maintaining a juvenile tone while we're doing the show. We are anything but adults when doing our podcast and, truthfully, I love it. We both relish the time together every week where we get to act like fifth graders.

Our audience has become our associate producers, sending in the most horrifying and silly content that the internet can provide. Once you tell a large audience that you like this sort of thing— you'd better hold on to your seat, because they are going to go beyond what you've seen or imagined. The email account is so active that I had to remove it from my phone. It averages more than 2,500 messages a week from listeners wanting to share their stories, songs, and the clips that I crave.

With Drew we had earmarked our favorites of the past six months: a man asking for a tattooed woman to beat him, a woman bathing in her own menstrual blood, a man encouraging people with ED to try meth because it helped him. You get the picture. As I ran through the clips with Drew, he kept shaking his head. "What do you like about this?"

I thought for a moment. "I like studying human behavior." I sat back with a smug smile on my face. Drew can't judge me now. My interest is purely academic and a fellow scholar will respect that. But Drew didn't accept it. He shot back, "You don't like studying human behavior, Tom."

I don't? I panicked. Was this doctor about to reveal my brain is actually poisoned? Does he know precisely what is wrong with me? *How* does he know?

"You like *abnormal* human behavior." My head dropped and I turned red. He was right, and he noticed the change in me. "You feel shame. Why?"

I *did* feel shame. I'd been exposed. What is wrong with me? Why does watching these clips fill me with happiness? Why do I laugh when I watch other people watch *those clips* for the first time? It's hard to describe, but when I press play I know something is about to happen. It's like a chef who knows he's going to feed someone Japanese A5 wagyu beef for the first time. There's really only two ways it can go, and both have "holy shit" in them. I want guests to either laugh or be vocally, physically uncomfortable.

I've always had a visceral reaction to strange behavior. People who don't know how to behave in a public setting are fascinating to me. I don't think I'm alone in that. When someone starts yelling and cursing in a restaurant or store, we all turn our heads and watch the chaos unfold. I've also always laughed uncontrollably when someone tells me a story of personal injury. I know it sounds awful, and I've presumed it's my way of dealing with something uncomfortable that I never knew how to process. When I was a little kid I would squirm at any gory details and eventually I would just laugh.

I knew that I was laughing a little too hard when I was working a construction job one summer in Florida and listened to a man tell a story about when he was injured. I was eighteen, and this was some brutal grunt work remodeling apartments with no AC. My friend Steve and I worked under a guy in his forties named Alan. Alan looked like he'd had somewhat of a rough life, rougher than ours for sure. He was thin, tan, and polite, but he had that *Florida man* vibe. He'd probably drifted all over the state and maybe even the entire southeast. Every morning we would arrive on-site and he would take us through the tasks of the day: painting, laying tile, hauling two-by-fours, etc. On one particularly hot day Alan removed his shirt and I saw something I had never seen before: a foreign object was protruding from inside his abdominal area. It was clearly something mechanical in nature, and it was *under* his skin!

"What the fuck is that, dude?"

"Oh, that's a morphine drip pouch."

"Huh?"

Alan went on to explain that the device I saw sticking out from his midsection was a port of morphine. It had a line from the port to his neck, where it would release a timed dosage. I had never seen or heard of anything like that, and in over twenty years to this day, I've only heard one person mention a similar device. When I asked Alan why he needed a morphine drip in his neck, I was unprepared for his straightforward answer.

"A bathtub fell on my neck from a third-floor window."

To say that I laughed would not be truthful. I went into an uncontrollable fit of laughter that was so powerful it rode on the verge of a seizure. My abs ached, and tears poured down my face. I tried to hide it at first, but it was so overwhelming that there wasn't a point in trying to pretend it wasn't happening. When I finally recovered, I sat up and looked at Alan. He had almost the same deadpan expression on his face but with a hint of a smirk. "That's... funny to you?"

I tried to explain then what I'm more capable of explaining now. It was the perfect storm of hilarity for me. It was the whole package: Alan's plain-faced expression, the unheard-of sewn-in opioid pouch, and the completely outrageous explanation that a bathtub fell on his neck from three stories up. It's exactly what is so great about a perfectly executed joke: the information of the joke coupled with the timing. Alan got me that day. Thankfully, he wasn't offended. He actually grew to enjoy my laughter at his pain, and he would show up some days and walk up to me. "I got one I think you'll like. I ever tell you about the time I broke both collarbones falling off a ladder?" I would collapse over listening to every horrible detail.

Fast-forward twenty years, and I still find something so funny about injuries. I have to make a clear distinction—I don't want to see them. I don't like open wounds or gore of any kind, but an injury story or video of one without gruesome footage will make me laugh. I swear that I don't fully understand why it makes me laugh, but it does.

One of our all-time most popular clips from *YMH* is captured from inside a car in Taiwan. The driver pulls into a mechanic's shop and the audio suggests that his car is manual and he is definitely anything but an expert at driving it. He is revving the engine hard and struggling to gracefully bring it into the garage. Another man is standing there, wearing dark coveralls and reading whatever is on his clipboard. He doesn't bother to look up until...the car hits him. The clipboard goes flying and the man lets out an almost inhuman yell: "Baaaaaaaa!!" He then yells commands in Mandarin, which we have since learned are the word "stuck." The driver doesn't move the car for more than a beat, so it makes sense that the mechanic is telling him that he's stuck. Finally, the car inches forward and the mechanic falls to the ground, moaning. The driver casually walks back, looks down at him with no expression on his face, and then...just walks away. I'll interrupt my justification for laughing to inform you that the man who was hit by the car made a full recovery—not even a broken bone. It was widely reported in Taiwan, so if you're holding on for, "Yeah, but what happened to that man?" Well, he's fine.

Back to the video. I would take the witness stand to defend my stance that this video is nothing short of hilarious; I've shown it to at least a dozen guests on our show, and I can happily report that a few agree. Some laugh just as hard as I did, and some look like their soul escaped when viewing it. I'm certain that it's funny. No doubt about it. But seriously, is something wrong with me?

If you're reading this you probably made it through 2020. Unless you're reading this hundreds of years from now. Nobody alive at this time can recall a year like 2020. There was a global pandemic, horrific humanitarian and economic consequences unlike any that we could imagine. I was so lucky that I got into podcasting ten years earlier and had built a fan base that wanted to consume what we were making. Everything was growing in that business, and it allowed us to thrive in the most depressing of years. I had made it almost through the entire year, not only unscathed but prospering. Could this historically bad year go any better for me? It was December 1, 2020. Literally the first day of the last month of that terrible year. My good friend Bert Kreischer and I were going to film some content for the livestreaming New Year's Eve podcast that we had planned. Bert and I do a weekly podcast called *2 Bears, 1 Cave* that has grown into one of the world's biggest comedy shows. We had done livestreaming podcasts before and really enjoyed putting them together. We had competed on the previous one by playing tennis. I trained for months after not having played for years. I got my forehand to a pretty good place and I was playing three days a week in anticipation of kicking my friend's ass. I knew he wasn't training as much as me. The only thing up in the air was, How good was his game back in the day? We had established that we both played tennis as teens, but you really never know the extent to which somebody was good twenty-five years ago. If there's one thing I can say about Bert, it's that he has a tendency for gross exaggerations. I was pretty confident that this was another one of his tall tales. He beat the shit out of me. 6–2, 6–1. It was demoralizing. My coach, Mike, whom I had worked with for months preparing for the match, was equally astounded. He pulled me aside and told me that Bert had a "legit Division I college serve." He also pointed out that he'd never seen such a discrepancy between someone's serve and the rest of their game. But it didn't matter. Bert's serve was so advanced I didn't have a chance.

I knew that on the next challenge I had to show him up. I needed to pick a sport or challenge where I felt extremely confident that I could return the favor to my friend. I chose basketball.

I actually played a lot of basketball earlier in my life. Pickup games, organized basketball, club basketball, and I always had a hoop in every house growing up. In college I would go to the gym and get in on games with some pretty good players. After moving to Los Angeles it was one of the first social activities I took part in. I would go to the Hollywood YMCA and get in on games there. Funny thing about saying the "Hollywood YMCA" is that people outside of Los Angeles think you mean the "show-biz YMCA" as if there are red carpets, Botox treatments in the lobby, and actors parading around in costumes. Angelenos know the truth. "Hollywood" means dirty, grimy, scrappy. Hollywood is easily one of the nastiest, most neglected parts of the city. It's filthy, and the pickup games are pretty good. I knew Bert didn't have the same basketball background as me. I chose this competition just to annihilate him.

That day we went to a private gym and were joined by You-Tube sensation and exceptionally talented basketball player Tristan Jass. He was a week shy of his twenty-first birthday. Tristan has built an enormous following by posting videos of himself playing basketball against bigger, faster opponents and not only holding his own, but often humiliating them. He also has an incredible ability to make trick shots that seem physically impossible.

First, we played Tristan 2 v 1, meaning Tristan had to play against the two of us. It's completely unfair to play two on one in basketball, since the team with two players can pass to each other, and the other team can only guard one at a time. On top of that we agreed that each basket that Bert and I scored would count as two points, while Tristan's baskets would count as one.

He beat us.

Totally Bert's fault for missing a wide-open layup. In case it isn't clear, Bert is fat and very bad at basketball.

After the game it was time for our preplanned dunk contest. It was a simple plan. Lower the hoop to seven feet, five inches, both of us attempt to dunk, and then incrementally raise the rim. Whoever can dunk on the highest height wins. We go back and forth until we get to nine feet. This was honestly kind of the goal for my old ass. I was saying that I was certain I could do it, but I had a little doubt. So did some of the staff in my office. They placed bets.

Bert went first. He came up just short and was certain he was done.

"I can't. Can't do it."

This was my big chance. I wanted to win this, then play Bert one on one and redeem myself for losing at tennis. I lined up and *boom*—dunked on nine feet. Forty-one years old and over 240 pounds. Truthfully, I was happy. I won the competition, and even my buddy Bert noted that it was "seriously impressive."

I felt good and was ready to move on, but then I heard it. Someone said, "I think you can go higher." I stopped. I really felt like nine feet was *close* to my limit. I had a bit of room, so maybe what, two, three inches more? Now the pressure felt like it was on. They raised the hoop to nine foot three. Roy, the man who worked at the gym and coached basketball, pulled me aside. He told me to dig deep on this attempt. I felt an adrenaline surge. My heart started to race. I started at the three-point line and began the stutter step to get my footing right. I got closer and pushed off my left leg. Almost immediately I heard and felt an explosion in my leg. It was quick and powerful. Like a gunshot. I didn't know what happened.

Did a car just hit me?

I didn't know if I was one or twenty-five inches off the ground. I knew I was falling back. My left arm instinctively went behind my back, and as I hit the court I felt the full impact on that arm. I knew immediately—it was broken.

I lay on my right side writhing in pain, moaning. I tried to pull my left arm close to my chest, but it was spun around and facing the wrong way behind me. Bert got close and twisted my arm back into place. I knew I was super fucked, and I just blurted out, "Call 911."

It wasn't long before it hit me. We were rolling multiple cameras.

"I'm going to be one of the videos I usually play."

A young baller who would be known for his basketball skills one day.

And boy, was I ever. We have multiple angles of my patellar tendon rupturing, humerus breaking, and me groaning in pain. It's pain porn. To be clear, and I think this is an important distinction, my video is not the kind of video that I would have laughed hysterically at. I say that and people assume, "Oh, because *you're* the one getting hurt, so now it's not so funny?" No, not at all. My criteria for what I involuntarily laugh at in these videos is pretty well documented. Sports injuries do not do it for me. They never have. I remember seeing Tim Krumrie's leg break in Super Bowl XXIII—nauseating. Willis McGahee in the 2003 Fiesta Bowl—gross. Dak Prescott in 2020—Jesus. They're all awful. That is not to say that one shouldn't laugh at my injury. Many have, and I fully accept it. I'm just pointing out that I'm not being a hypocrite. But back to my video—oh, *boy*, did people *love* it. I knew it would get some views, but, Jesus Christ, it took over my life in every way.

Physically I was completely incapable of doing the most menial task for almost a month. The double whammy of arm and leg being severely injured meant that even after surgery I would need to be tended to by professionals to do *everything*: eat, drink, sit, stand, and, of course, wipe. I don't think there's a more undignified line that can come from your mouth than, "I'm done pooping. Can you wipe me?" To be fair I met the most amazing nurses, who only made me feel dignified and respected, but still. At forty-one you don't imagine you'll actually *need* someone to wipe your shitty ass. One male nurse actually didn't want to, but let's forgive him. I wouldn't want to wipe my ass either if I saw me. I clearly remember the moment I went back to wiping myself. I had shit, called out that I was done, and a shift change had occurred between nurses. The older nurse left while I was still pushing, and the cute nurse took over. When she walked up to me as I sat on the toilet I looked up and thought, *Naw, I can't let her.*

The video of my injury is now unavoidable if you search my name on any platform. The footage was set to debut as a pay-per-view event on my YMHstudios.com site. It wasn't the only thing planned for the big New Year show, but clearly it was the main attraction. We knew people would want to see it and expected a solid turnout, but it far surpassed our expectations. My fans knew how I got hurt, but this gave them a chance to see it. So many people bought tickets that we crashed the streaming site, but it was after the show that the real show began.

First people posted the clip of my injury; then the memes, deep fakes, Photoshops, and even toy figurines took over. Yes, yours truly has a limited edition run of handmade mini figures of me, just what I dreamed of as a child, only these have me in the fetal position, grimacing and with a broken, twisted arm.

The videos were posted and reposted thousands of times. I was the top gif search, trending on social media, and talked about by sports shows. At times it was overwhelming. I literally couldn't get away from the footage or reactions to it. When the dust finally settled, I had to ask myself, had this experience changed me? There's no way I could sit here and tell you that it had not. It has changed me in so many ways: physically, mentally, and emotionally. It was a truly traumatic event. Those stay with you. Yes, you're able to continue living your life, but the scar, or in this case the scars, they'll always be there. They'll serve as quiet reminders of what happened that day and how it was, hopefully, the beginning of a new you. So it begs the question: Do I still laugh when I see a video of someone getting hurt?

Absolutely.

Save the Word

This morning I was running late because I slept in. Not like in the old days, before we had children. Back then sleeping *in* meant *into* the afternoon. Those days are long gone. These days "sleeping in" means anything past 7:00 a.m. My oldest son, Ellis, is six. He likes staying up late and waking up early, the perfect recipe for ruining *your* day. He also wakes up ready for whatever, shot out of a cannon. He usually shouts "Come smell my ass" first thing in the morning until you go to his room and greet him or he'll run into our room, pull his pants down, bend over, spread his butt cheeks, and say, "I had a nightmare."

Yeah, I think I'm looking at it.

His younger brother, Julian, is three. He'll change his sleep cycle every week and you just have to adapt. One week he'll sleep twelve hours and take no naps, the next week he'll sleep ten hours a night and take an hour nap after pre-K at home; oh, and he'll nap in the car, and if you disturb *that* nap you'll pay the price with your sanity as he will cry and fight you for disturbing him. The next week he's sleeping eight hours a night with no naps. It's a ride.

So today I got up late because these two maniacs woke me up separately at different hours when I should have been sleeping. The older one, Ellis, came in at one-thirty a.m. to say he had peed in bed. I changed his pajamas and then he said, "Come change my sheets." I tried to get him to sleep on a bath towel.

"I don't like towels."

Fine. I changed his sheets and basically woke all the way up to do so. Eventually, I went back to sleep. Next, the younger one, Julian, woke up crying. I pretended not to hear it so my wife would take care of him, and she did. That was at 3:30 a.m. Then at 5:30 a.m. he did it again, and since we take turns with them, she violently shook me and said the dreaded words, "Your turn."

I rocked him, but it was too late or too early, however you want to see it. He was up. I felt like my eyes were bleeding. I got back in bed and then overslept. It felt like no time had passed, but it was almost 8:00 a.m. and I needed to take Ellis to school. I had everything ready to go—his backpack, lunch, water bottle, keys, wallet, phone—but I was forgetting my most important accessory for leaving the house: sunglasses. I mean it. I'd rather not eat for a week than not have sunglasses. You see, Jesus loves me. I know this because he gave me blue eyes. Blue like the heavens above. And yes, you might get lost staring into my dreamy, water-hued eyeballs, but you should know that they only despise one thing: bright lights. You, reading this, probably don't have blue eyes, right? You probably have turd eyes. Brown, diarrhea-colored eyes are very common. I frown all day whenever I see them. "Caca eyes," as they are referred to in the medical community, might look like shit when you see them, but the one and only upside of having those poop balls in your head is that they process light much more effectively. If I don't have sunglasses, my eyes actually hurt and so does my head. I just want to lie down without them. So now I'm panicking. I'm running around, trying to leave, but I *have* to have my sunglasses or else the bright morning sun will blind me. I stop at the door, exasperated. I know I'm leaving without them when I see my wife, who is late for work herself.

"Hey."

"Whatever it is, the answer is 'No.'"

"Please."

"No."

"I need your help."

"The kids are in the car. I'm not going to fuck you."

"No, not that!"

"What, what is it?!"

"Have you seen my sunglasses?"

She stops. Looks dead into my perfect eyes, and then I note a telling smirk on her face. She knows something.

She reached up and grabbed them off the top of my head and handed them to me.

"I'm retarded."

She agreed, "You are the *most* retarded. But I love you."

Here you were thinking you were reading a warm, relatable story about parenting. You're not. It's me complaining that I want to say words that some people have deemed unacceptable. Now, maybe you're saying, "*Seriously, Tom, get with the times. The world evolves and you need to evolve with it, you dinosaur.*"

I agree. I really think we should all move forward as there is no point in fighting change and progress, so I should make it clear that there aren't a series of words and phrases that I'm holding on to. It's really just one.

Retarded.

Every year the world changes in numerous ways. We've never seen change like we saw in 2020. Not in my lifetime, and from what I gather, the wave of protests and unrest are even more significant than what happened in 1968, when a devastating war and civil rights demonstrations dominated the psyche of the American public. One change that we're not always ready for is language. Words that once were the norm become antiquated and sometimes offensive. We as a society weigh the suggested substitute and act...or we don't. It used to be okay to say "Oriental" to describe a person from Asia. Some time in recent years that changed. Although the word is still used to describe objects such as rugs and businesses such as hotels, it is unacceptable to use it when describing a person. Most have accepted that standard. You can tell it's not really an issue because you rarely hear the term "Oriental" in conversation when describing a person, unless the person talking is over eighty, and in that case, the person you are speaking with is about to die.

"That Oriental lady sure is pretty."

"Grandpa, that's your doctor and you have Alzheimer's."

If people really wanted to say "Oriental" when describing an Asian person, you'd hear arguments for it all the time. Your friends would constantly bring it up.

"I just don't get why she's upset. She was *Oriental* and a lot of them do that for tips. What's the problem?"

But you never hear that. No one complains because no one is married to saying that. The adjustment period is over, if there ever was one.

"Retarded" is different. Not only is the history of the word different. The current-day hypocrisy around it is astounding. People say "retarded" online and in conversation because we reject the notion that the term is outdated. What is true is that proclaiming that the word is not acceptable is en vogue. People will rant and rave, as they have to me, that we cannot say it as it hurts those with developmental disabilities, even though it is widely accepted to have a second and much more popular definition.

Do you believe the Sandy Hook shooting was fake and that the US didn't really land on the moon in 1969? Have you responded to an email asking you to verify your personal information or password without questioning who sent it? Do you expel infinite energy and time engaging strangers online in tweets or posts about sports/politics/culture when you could be hugging your kids/eating a croissant/making love to your partner? Do you freak out and curse when you can't find your sunglasses only to discover they're on your head? Well, in each of those cases you were being retarded.

I don't like the word "retarded." I *love* it. I think it's my absolute favorite word in the English language. It's perfect. I understand that a lot of people don't like it, but I also understand that those people are the worst. Let's be honest, *most* of them are retarded. Not literally, of course, and that seems to be where at least part of the issue lies. You say "retarded" and people think that you mean *mentally* retarded. "Mentally retarded" is a medical term from the early twentieth century. At the time it was used to describe those with developmental disabilities. Naturally, the term could be used to insult someone who had said or done something foolish. But over the next 100 years it evolved to have a second, more widely used definition. That definition is essentially silly, preposterous, or thoughtless. It's said without malice or venom and it's said by millions, even those who lecture you not to say it. I know this from firsthand experience. I've had very well-meaning friends and associates sit me down and explain how hurtful it is to use a word that is so damaging when they can think of so many other words that summarize what I want to say without saying it. These lectures would give me pause as I wondered what I should start saying to replace the perfect word and *then*, as if the lord had sent the message himself, days and sometimes weeks later the person and I will be having a conversation about life, in one case about a party this person had been to, and then *boom*, they dropped it without thinking.

"Todd went on a run and brought back bottles of beer in a paper bag, and when he got back he leaned over the balcony to drop them down to me. He dropped sixty bottles of beer *from a balcony.*"

"Why would he do that?"

"He's retarded."

I didn't get mad. I didn't even call him out. He was right. That's exactly how I would describe Todd too.

It should be noted that this is different than calling someone a *retard*. That has a lot more sting to it, and when you say *that* to someone, you're just being mean. I'm not telling you when not to be mean, but if you thought you could grab a piping-hot cast iron skillet with a paper towel, well, you know what you are.

The word is perfect. Not just for me; for you too. If you're someone who only thinks that the word is pejorative, cruel, and meant to attack those who cannot defend themselves I would urge you to reconsider. Might you familiarize yourself with my good friend, Bert Kreischer. He cohosts the podcast *2 Bears, 1 Cave* with me. It's a weekly podcast where we sit around, talk shit, and laugh. But if you really want to break it down, it's basically Bert regurgitating an endless stream of words that are tethered together only by the fact that he's saying them. He switches topics faster than he finishes beers. He typically will run through half a dozen brews in an hour. My role is trying to make sense of it, any of it. Bert is one-of-a-kind. He bathes in his swimming pool. This is a grown man who brings shampoo into his pool when it's time to "shower." He runs three to five miles a day, five days a week, on a treadmill. But he doesn't just run them, he drinks a box of wine while he runs. He cuts his toenails and tapes them to the underside of his living room coffee table. Do I need to go on? He's a great guy and one of the best friends you could ask for. He's loyal, genuine, and absolutely hilarious. If you asked me to describe him, I'd tell you all those things I listed and more. I love him with all my heart, but truthfully, and I mean this from the heart, if I were to describe him I'd have to include another word. Retarded.

Photo Essay

1. *Studies have shown that it's harder to get mad at someone when you have pictures of them as a child. If something in this book upsets you, look at this photo. Such a sweet, innocent boy who wouldn't be corrupted for years. Still mad at me?*

2. *This is my favorite photo of my mother. She's leaning forward on the sofa, her left hand by her ankle. Her best friend, Charo Figari, is looking at her with such affection you can feel it. My mom's sister, Blanca, is on the ground in front of them. Also, I love the smoking. It really is the coolest, and I wish more people smoked.*

3. *My dad (front row, center) aka Top Dog with the platoon he led in Vietnam. Oorah!*

4. *My parents loved cruises.*

5. *They made us go on a lot of them. That's not someone I "experimented" with. That's my cousin Brian and we've been happily together for forty-two years.*

6. *This is Charlie. Great friend I met in college. Also was the best man at my wedding.*

7. *As a comedian I feel obligated to include the worst photo I could find of myself. This was on a cruise during spring break in college. My roommates, Casey and Justin, were with me. They were also not sober here.*

8. *"What?"*

9. *This photo is dedicated to my Sudaca brothers and sisters. The photo was taken in Madrid at a restaurant that this lovely woman owned and operated. The food was great, but I took a photo with her because her name was Concha. Jajaja. I triple checked and even had her spell it.*

10. *When I go abroad I try to blend in. Tunisia with my dad was a blast.*

11. *This was my favorite dog ever. Feefo was his name, and he was a rescue, so I'm actually a really great person.*

12. *This is what doing stand-up usually looks like and what I normally played to for the first twelve years: a small room with a few people and we're all just trying to make them laugh.*

13. *With my best buddy Bart Krisinger.*

14. *I've really done it all.*

15. *When my wife, Christina P., and I do a live podcast in a city we travel to, we try to dress like the locals. This was in Palm Beach, Florida, so country club douchebags it was!*

16. *What 90 percent of working the road looks like.*

17. *I can't believe it either.*

Mike Tyson

American Airlines 1704, LAX to PIT, 2:17 p.m.

It's one thing to meet a celebrity. It's entirely another to meet an icon: someone so famous that people from all walks of life, all ages and ethnicities, seem to lose their sense of how to behave like normal humans when they encounter him. I witnessed this personally the day I flew from Los Angeles to Pittsburgh on the same flight as Mike Tyson.

Young passengers stopped in the aisle. "No shit!"

"I love *The Hangover*!"

An older lady making her way to her seat simply paused as her mouth hung open, speechless. And a *lot* of dudes bowed down to the ultimate alpha male. "Hey, champ!" "You're the man, Mike!" The guys raised their fists, acknowledging that they know Mike's fist is *the* fist.

Tyson's assistant, Rashad, once told me that when they visited China—one of the most strict, regimented countries on the planet—even the customs agents at the airport all left their posts to grab a photo with him. *Customs agents in China* are probably the last people on earth I would guess to be swayed by celebrities, but this is Mike Tyson. He's lived a life that most of us can't even conceive of, and most of it has been in front of our eyes: triumph, defeat, tragedy, comedy, hope, and despair all wrapped up in a pit bull's body with an unmistakable lisp. You might have noticed that I mentioned talking to Tyson's assistant, and you're probably wondering how that came to be. Well, I, like all the other passengers, was fascinated by the champ's presence, and I couldn't help myself. More on that soon.

The first time I heard his name I was six or seven years old. I don't remember which fight it was, I just remember my dad complaining that "this guy" kept knocking people out in the first round, and my dad was pissed that it was over so quickly.

"Shit! There goes fifty bucks. What was that, twenty seconds?"

I thought it was awesome, but it wasn't my money spent on the pay-per-view.

I didn't really understand why my dad wasn't happy to have the fight end after one minute. I thought this dude was like a character that had popped out of a comic book, a superhero among us mere mortals on earth. I mean, he sure looked like one. Mike was compact and muscular. His torso looked like it was chiseled from stone. He had the most menacing eyes on his way to the ring, but hey, he wasn't mad at me, so I loved watching him terrify *other* people. Later, I learned he was called "Iron" Mike Tyson aka "The Baddest Man on the Planet." To me he looked like the baddest man on *any* planet. You think anyone on Mars wants a piece of Mike?

I followed the epic saga that is his life with devoted interest like when a new season of *Ozark* drops on Netflix. So the last thing I imagined is that I would someday have the opportunity to meet this global icon.

I shouldn't have ever met him. When I say I should never have met him, I really mean it. I was supposed to sit in coach that day, but I was upgraded last minute at the gate. I boarded with the first few people, and at the time it didn't seem unlike the thousands of other flights I've boarded. People are tired, most are dressed casually, which is a nice way of saying terribly. People used to wear suits to fly; now it looks like they're picking up a sixer at 7-Eleven before they get back to their bonfire on the beach, wearing flip-flops and tank tops. You see the sensible business traveler, always wearing a shirt tucked in, with monogrammed luggage tags, letting people know, "I fly...*a lot*." I watched this normal parade of passengers walk past me and then I saw him. I looked up, then down, but my head shot back up, realizing what my eyes had just seen. Mike Tyson walked right past me and sat one row behind me, across the aisle in the aisle seat. At the time I was in the window seat, and there was one other guy in my row, seated on the aisle. The row in front of us was completely empty, so I suggested the aisle guy move up so we could each have a row to ourselves. This was, admittedly, completely calculated on my part. I wanted to sit *that* much closer to Mike and increase the possibility of talking to him. The guy sitting next to me never noticed. He was a total "Justin."

Over the next hour, I plotted how I would approach him. I had listened to the two old boners behind me force conversation with him, and it was excruciating. One of them asked him if he "remembered" one of his championship fights, because this man also remembered it. I was fuming quietly at what douchebags these guys were. The other offered him lunch the next day at his restaurant. I thought long and hard and decided I wouldn't try to be cool. I'd just be sincere and possibly humiliated. I reached into my bag and pulled out a shrink-wrapped DVD of my first special, *Completely Normal*. The plan was to pass it off, like a mixtape. I got myself together, stood up, and slowly took the few steps back to Mike. He looked up at me, and I have to admit I was really nervous. Do you remember asking the girl you thought was pretty to dance in middle school? Your heart races, your throat dries out, and you stammer through the words. It's a terrifying experience. This was like that, only this time the pretty girl was known as The Baddest Man on the Planet, and he could use his fists to kill you if he didn't want to dance. Still, I tried to remain composed as my voice cracked a bit and my mind wondered if I was upsetting him by talking to him.

"Hey, Mike. I'm a big fan. My name's Tom Segura and I'm a comedian. This is a DVD of my special."

I presented my DVD to him, still shrink-wrapped. He took it and, much to my surprise, actually looked at it for a moment, then he looked at me and began speaking.

"You're a comedian?"

"Yeah, I'm going to Pittsburgh to do shows. What about you?"

"I'm going to promote a fight."

"Oh, cool."

"I hate fights."

"Oh." I wasn't sure how to respond or what he meant, but he elaborated.

"Fighting is so chaotic and brings up so many emotions in me. I'd rather avoid it, but I gotta pay the bills."

One of my favorite things about Mike over the years is witnessing how self-aware, introspective, and philosophical he'd become. Here I was, getting my own little display of this, and I was loving every second of it.

"Where's your show?"

"It's a comedy club called the Pittsburgh Improv."

"Where's that?"

"I'm...not sure." I mean I'm still not sure. I rarely know the exact location of any comedy club in the nation. I just travel to these cities and know the name of the club. The club always arranges transportation for the headlining comic, so we really never know specifics unless we're very curious. Also, what if I did know the neighborhood? Would that actually mean something to Mike Tyson? Is he familiar with Pittsburgh's neighborhoods? "Hey, the club is in West Homestead, across from Somerset." Like now he's going to say, "Oh, off 376 on the waterfront? Yeah, I love it there."

Then he asked what might be my favorite question of our whole interaction.

"Is your show tonight?"

He asked this as we were still on a plane, close to 11:00 p.m. eastern time. What time would my show be, 2:00 a.m.?

"Uh, no. It's tomorrow."

"Where?"

"The...Pittsburgh Improv."

"How do I find it?"

This one left me frozen for a second. Mike's stare is an intense one. I watched him stare down his opponents before they fought so many times—even from my living room I could see the fear in their eyes. Now, here I was, standing above him, and I could feel a hint of that stare. Suddenly I'm Michael Spinks, and the worst moment of my life is about to happen. He had just asked me a question, and his expression said, "You'd better know the answer." I just blurted out whatever words popped into my mind.

"Well, if you Google my name, which is on the DVD, it'll bring up my calendar and then you can see where I'm performing. That's probably the best way to find it."

He thanked me and I went back to my seat. I was breathing

extra hard as every ounce of me had been clearly suppressing how
nervous I felt to engage him. But I did it. I was proud of myself. Just
as my heart rate was coming down, I heard his unmistakable voice.

"Tooooom."

I turned and Tyson was looking at me, casually twisting my
DVD in his hands. "Were you on television recently?" I thought
for a second, wishing the answer was *yes*, but knowing it was not.
"No. Uh-uh."

"You sure?"

"Yeah. I mean . . . Yeah."

"Nothing?"

I thought for a beat and casually dropped, "I mean, I'm on
Netflix."

"*Hell, yeah!* I love Netflix! What's your favorite show on Netflix, Tom?"

I tell him *Breaking Bad* even though I know it's not a Netflix
show. I'm nervous and I also want him to think what I watch is a
solid choice. Without hesitating he says, "Yeah, my wife likes that."

Gutted. He said it like, "Some people like the ballet."

Then his eyes lit up. "You like *Sons of Anarchy*?" I was dev-
astated. I'd heard friends and critics rave about the show for
years, but I'd never seen a single frame of it. It's just one of those
things—there are only so many shows you can watch. Now I had
the champ looking at me with boyish wonder in his eyes and I had
to say something. Do I disappoint him more? Of course not.

"My favorite fuckin' show."

Mike let out a maniacal laugh. "I knew you with it! That shit's
wild!" He extended his fist, a fist that has ruined so many faces
and nights for opponents. It sat there in the open space of the aisle
looking like a goddamn sledgehammer. I extended my baby fist

and gave him a bump. Awesome. This could not have gone any better. I not only met Mike, gave him my special and had a friendly chat, but we had a real moment. Even though I lied, it was worth it.

Now I was facing forward again and beaming, reliving the last ten minutes of this flight over and over. I was anxious to land so I could call my friends.

Just as my breathing returned to normal, I felt a strong grip on my left shoulder. It honestly felt like what I imagine a DEA agent's grasp would feel like when they finally got their hands on El Chapo. It had big "stay right where you are" energy. I turned around expecting someone of authority to be looking over my shoulder, but it was Mike. His expression was nonchalant. This was simply a "greeter's grasp" to him, I presume. I had no idea what was about to happen. Tyson standing over you with his hand on your shoulder is a major alpha position. My eyes widened a bit, as did my mouth, and my asshole followed. Without warning he leaned down to my left ear and gently whispered.

"I've been watching a lot of Netflix."

That's it. Then he stood up and he was looking at me like, "It's your turn to talk."

I stammered a bit but managed to say, "Me too. They have... so many things to watch."

"I recognize you." He held up the DVD I had given him. "This is the same picture that's on Netflix."

For a brief moment I wasn't sure if he was fucking with me. He was showing me a picture of me that I had *just* given him and mentioning that it was on Netflix after I had *just* said that. But the look on his face was sincere, kind, and hopeful.

"Oh yeah, that's the copy of that special."

"I know who you are." This was surreal. Beyond surreal,

actually. This larger-than-life figure who I grew up watching knock out grown men like he was in a video game was looking at me telling me he knows me.

"What's your phone number?

"Mine?"

Rashad, the man who had been sitting next to Mike, pulled out his phone. I gave him my number.

"We comin' to your show tomorrow." It was Mike's last statement to me before returning to his seat.

Soon after, we landed and I hurried off the plane. It felt like the interaction had gone so well that any staying behind could only ruin it. I didn't want to overstay my welcome.

On the way to my hotel I called three friends and my father. I had to tell people. All of them responded with disbelief.

"Kid Dynamite!"

"You've made it, Tommy!"

"Did he make you suck his dick?"

That last one came from my friend Casey, not my father.

The next morning I woke up thinking it was a dream and *knowing* that, as with a lot of celebs, many of whom I had encountered, I would never see him again. Sure, he said he wanted to come to the show, but everyone knows that is just something people say. And it's not limited to celebrities. Most of the time it's non-celebs, if I'm being honest. People constantly ask when and where your shows are and make proclamations about how they "definitely" want to come and how they're "trying" to make it as if it's meaningful to you, the performer, if they do or not. Little do they know, most comics not only don't care, they sometimes dread people they actually know coming to the show.

I decided to take a chance. I was going to tell the club to maybe

expect Mike Tyson to come to the show. Why not? No one would know except for the guy I was telling, and he was the manager of a comedy club, so fuck him. I called. I was nervous.

"Uh, yeah, I'm at the hotel... Yeah all good... Show's at seven? Okay, cool... one other thing... Mike Tyson... might come to the show tonight."

"The fighter?"

"No, the guy who founded Tyson Chicken. Yeah, the fighter."

The manager paused. "Holyfield too?"

"Uh, I don't think so."

He told me if it happened they'd take care of him.

I wanted Mike to come, but more than that I wanted him to come to a *great* show. Most shows are fine, even good. Some are terrible beyond belief, and then some are just... magic. I was praying for one of those.

But in comedy, like life, things don't ever go how you think they will.

The afternoon felt like the longest one I could remember. I walked to a diner, paced around a mall, went to the gym, and stared at the ceiling in my hotel room. I couldn't believe how much the anticipation was fucking with me. I just wanted to know whether or not he'd really come to the show. Around 3:30 p.m. my phone rang.

"Tom, it's Mike Tyson. We comin' to your show tonight, brotha."

"Fuckin'...really?"

"Yeah, we wanna watch you do your work."

I was genuinely excited. "That's fuckin' crazy!"

He was gracious.

"It's all love."

I'd heard that expression before. It's one I really enjoy. You're simply stating that the action you are taking is all about the best thing in the world, love. In this case, brotherly love. I knew it was my turn to talk, and I wanted to say something that conveyed a similar message. I wanted to sound cool. I paused and then I said it.

"I love you."

Fuck. I shut my eyes so hard I almost had a stroke. *What am I doing? I just told Mike Tyson I love him?!* There was a pause on his end.

"Aight, good luck tonight," and the line went dead. Did I just ruin this? Was the former undefeated, undisputed heavyweight champion of the world about to come to my show, but changed his mind the moment I fell apart and professed my love to him?

The house was half full. I started and the first joke fell flat. I was distracted, looking for the champ. I kept doing my set, and then it happened. I heard a loud slapping of a table, I squinted and saw Mike Tyson about three quarters of the way back in the room. The show ended up being...*fine.* It was hard to concentrate because all I could think was, *Is Mike laughing at this? Am I bombing? Is he going to walk out?* Luckily, I couldn't clearly see him, and I was finishing my set strong, but all I could think about was, What happens next with Mike? Do I acknowledge him and ask him to stand so 183 people can say, "Are you shitting me?" Should I wave like a kid in a commercial to one of their sports idols? Luckily for me, I didn't have to think long. As I walked up the aisle, the audience was clapping and music played, and then I felt what I can only describe as what you might feel right before a polar bear effortlessly tears your shoulder off. Mike had slapped my back.

"Funny shit, Tom! Let's go to the green room!"

I didn't even say a word. I just followed Mike to *my* green room. He led the way, of course.

Once inside this small room, Mike and two of his crew got comfortable and Mike began smoking cigarettes. One after the other. One thing that amazed me about this was how one of the guys would light Mike's cig *as* he was putting it up to his lips. He didn't have to wait a beat. That was the first time in my life witnessing that level of...submissiveness. I mean it's beyond "baller." It's a guy making sure you don't blink between cigarettes. Something I imagine Prince Al-Waleed bin Talal would have had done for him in one of his *three* Saudi palaces, should the multi-billionaire investor decide to begin smoking.

The conversation with Mike was epic. I'd love to put it all in this book, but I would certainly fear for my safety and ability to chew solid foods if I divulged all the details. I can say that we talked life, boxing, and a lot of Mike's ups and downs. One of my favorite moments that I feel like I can share is how he viewed his role when stepping into the ring. He said it wasn't just about beating his opponent, but respecting that the audience wants to see a "show."

He was going for those knockouts, not just to win, but because he knew we wanted to see them. I loved it! He also went into detail about boxers he didn't think respected the audience and how boring they were to watch, and I will not be listing those names here!

After about his fourth cigarette, he asked me, "You got a window in here?" I'm thinking, *It's a little late for that. You've been puffing for an hour.* I look around and tell him, "No, no window." And like something straight out of a movie, he took a long drag off his smoke and said, "That's when you'll know you've made it. When your green room has a window."

I'd never heard it put that way or thought about it, but it registered right away. It also felt like someone clearly telling me, "You *definitely* have not made it yet."

Mike smoked a few more cigs, then said he was going to turn in. A few hours had passed, and when I opened the door to walk him out, the entire staff of the club was lined up. They all wanted pics, and Mike obliged.

If this story sounds familiar to you, it's because you've heard the stage version, one that I started telling the next day. It *killed* immediately. Eventually it became my closing bit on the new hour I was working on. You can see the stand-up version of it on my 2016 Netflix special, *Mostly Stories*. I also ended up telling it on talk shows and podcasts as it was a fan favorite. One random afternoon a few years later, I got a call from Joe Rogan. He told me to come by his studio in about an hour. When I walked in, I saw a group of people sitting in one of Joe's green rooms.

I made my way through the small gathering to see who was on the couch. It was Mike Tyson holding court. He looked up at me.

"Man, you know people stop me all the time, asking me if that shit is true. I say, 'Yeah, man. All that happened.'"

"Me too!"

He got up and gave me a hug, and I thought, what a cool moment. I thanked Joe and then Joe really surprised me. He leaned in and said in my ear, "Why don't you stay and podcast with us?"

My heart almost stopped. Not only was I floored at the offer, but I was torn as well. This happened to be the day that I was supposed to be meeting up with my wife at a hotel nearby to celebrate our anniversary. I didn't know what to say. What I felt was that even though sitting in on a podcast with Mike Tyson seemed like the coolest thing in the world, something about it made me feel like I shouldn't put it over my wife, especially on our anniversary. It felt like the right thing to do was leave. I didn't want to make that call: "Hey, I'm podcasting for a while so…see you later?" I told him I could stay for a little bit, but we got started and the podcast was awesome. I got to ask him something I had never remembered to ask when we hung out, which was, "What made you think you could get a tiger?" The answer was better than anything you could make up. Mike told a story about ordering his first wildcat from *prison*. He was on the phone with his car broker and the broker happened to mention that he could also get wild animals, so naturally Mike said, "Can I get a tiger?" And his car broker told him, "No problem." Mike Tyson basically got a tiger because his car guy was out of Bentleys.

The energy was flowing *so* well on this podcast, but I kept looking at the time. I needed to make a decision: stay and have a good talk or leave. I was feeling anxious and told the two of them, "I gotta go." And it was Mike who was pleading with me to stay.

"Come on, man. Don't go." Surreal. Iron Mike telling me to stay because he was having fun.

I had to.

"Wife, you know." They both nodded.

I left Joe's studio and had to pause.

Damn, that would have been cool to stay.

I took the 405 over the hill to the Beverly Hills Hotel. I arrived a few minutes before my wife and took her to their famous eatery, the Polo Lounge, for lunch. I tried to talk about anything else, but I couldn't stop thinking about what had just happened.

"You're not going to believe it. I was just podcasting with Joe and Mike Tyson. So unreal. But you know what, I left, so I could be here with you."

"Why didn't you stay?"

Umm, isn't it obvious? Hello?

"I didn't want you to feel bad that I made that a priority over meeting up on our anniversary."

Clearly there are big-time husband points to be had here. I stopped doing what I *wanted* to do because I was putting her first. Isn't that what every wife wants? For their husband to stop enjoying himself so he can have lunch with her.

"Oh...I would've stayed."

"What? But we had plans to be here...now."

"Yeah, but it's Mike Tyson."

GOD FUCKING DAMNIT.

Pulitzer Prize Submission

Wow, what a ride, huh? There's good literature, and then there's what you just finished reading. Hopefully, you have the confidence that you can make a pipe bomb in under an hour and without incriminating yourself. I mean that was the goal of this writing.

No! I'm just goofing around. I do feel like you probably have a better understanding of paleomagnetism and the conflict in Gaza. I'm able to see these complicated situations and make them easy to digest for you, the reader. But seriously, I am extremely thankful to you for purchasing or stealing this book and reading it. If you didn't read it and just flipped to this page, I commend you on your inability to start things. Hopefully, you laughed throughout or maybe even a few times. It'd be weird if you only laughed once, but still, that's better than not laughing at all. If you did buy this book and you read the whole thing and you never even let out a sound, I feel like you might have some sort of undiagnosed personality disorder. Check out the DSM and see what feels most like "you."

I'm going to dinner now, but it's going to be a sensible portion, so I don't get all super fat like my dear friend Bert.

Acknowledgments

It's easy to finish reading a masterpiece, as you just have, and think, *Wow, he did this all on his own?* And while it's true that I did write every word, I must acknowledge the amazing support system I have.

I was blessed to be raised by two amazing parents. My father, Tom, who passed shortly after this manuscript was handed in, was simply the best dad a kid could ever ask for. I miss him and am eternally grateful for everything he taught me. My mom, Rosario, who is simply the funniest person I've ever met, also raised me to be a gentleman, and though I constantly disappoint her, she knows I try. Also, I bought her a car today, the day I'm writing this, so whatever. I'd like to thank my completely insane sisters, Maria and Jane. They're incredibly loyal, loving, and also out of their minds. I wouldn't be who I am without my uncle Dave and aunt Blanca and their three children, my cousins: Michelle, Brian, and Jeanette.

I'm fortunate to have the most supportive wife in the world, without whom nothing I do would be possible. Thank you, Christina, for your love and dedication to our family. Huge love to my two little monsters: Ellis and Julian. They make every day an adventure, and I'll miss the day they stop arguing which is more famous: *Pac-Man* or *Cars*.

A mi familia Latina. Les quiero TANTO. Espero que les veo pronto. Son los mas amables y son mis tesoros. Gracias por todo.

I never would have attempted this if not for my rock star agent, Richard Abate. Thanks for the encouragement and always having my back. No, I'm not ready to do this again.

I never thought I'd actually look forward to someone's notes, but that was exactly the case with my editor, Suzanne O'Neill. You are brilliant, and I loved working with you, though I would have appreciated more deadline extensions.

Deep appreciation for the whole team at Grand Central and Hachette for your professionalism and attention to every detail.

Huge admiration for Elece Green for her top-tier directing of the audiobook.

My comedy friends, who make me laugh and always make me want to do better: Bert "Fat Sticks" Kreischer, Ryan Sickler, Geoff Tate, Joe Rogan, Ari Shaffir, Joey Diaz, Brian Simpson, Kirk Fox, and a couple dozen others whom I'm currently forgetting because I'm tired of writing this.

My A1 tour team: Dave Ockun, Shaun Nix, Kier Bailey, Marcus Johnson, and Rick Smith. These guys make my touring happen and helped immensely in this process.

Lastly, I must acknowledge the incredible team at YMH, whom I fortunate enough to work with every week: Nadav "Capital J" Itzkowitz, Enny "Hot Sauce" Moss, Ryan "Boss Man" Hall, Chris "Second Place" Larson, Josh "Baby J" Zollo, Chad "Smarter" Wallin, and Danny "Dumb Hair" Dimaso. You guys are the best.

I know I'm forgetting some people I should really thank, and I hope they'll forgive me. I love you all.

About the Author

Tom Segura is a comedian originally from Cincinnati, Ohio. Well-known for his Netflix specials *Ball Hog, Disgraceful, Completely Normal,* and *Mostly Stories,* he cohosts two of the most popular comedy podcasts, *Your Mom's House* with his wife, comedian Christina P., and *2 Bears, 1 Cave* with fellow comedian Bert Kreischer.